American
ENGLISH FILE

Workbook

Christina Latham Koenig
Clive Oxenden
with
Jane Hudson

Paul Seligson and Clive Oxenden are the original co-authors of
English File 1 and *English File 2*

OXFORD
UNIVERSITY PRESS

Contents

ONLINE SELF-ASSESSMENT MATERIAL

Powerful listening and interactive practice

The American English File Second Edition Download Center includes class audio, workbook audio, all video, and a Progress Check for each File.

- **AUDIO** – Download ALL of the audio files for the Listening and Pronunciation activities in this Workbook for on-the-go listening practice.
- **PRACTICE** – Check your progress by taking a self-assessment test after you complete each File.

AUDIO

When you see this symbol **ONLINE**, go to

www.oup.com/elt/americanenglishfile:

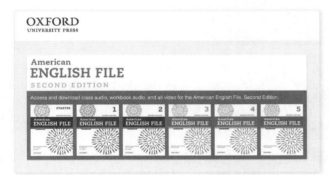

Choose the correct level or American English File.

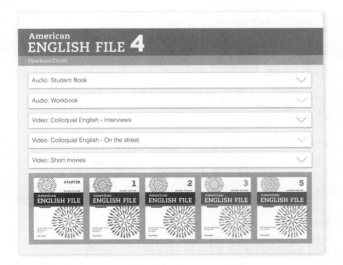

Choose **"Audio: Workbook."**

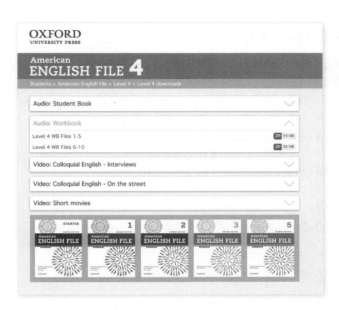

PRACTICE

At the end of every File, there is a Progress Check.

To do the Progress Check, select the File you have just finished.

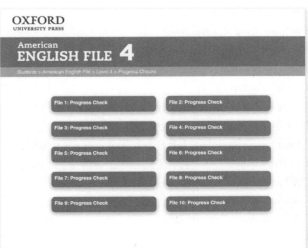

1A Questions and answers

1 GRAMMAR question formation

a Right (✔) or wrong (✗)? Correct the mistakes in the highlighted phrases.

1 **A** You have ever been to Thailand? **✗ *Have you ever been***
  B Yes, a couple of times.
2 **A** Why didn't you tell me the truth? **✔** _____
  B Because I thought you'd be angry.
3 **A** Where you usually go on vacation? _____
  B We usually go to Mexico.
4 **A** Haven't you done the homework? _____
  B No, I haven't. I'm sorry.
5 **A** What did happen at the meeting yesterday? _____
  B We discussed the sales figures. It was kind of boring.
6 **A** Who is Jack going out with? _____
  B He's going out with his best friend's sister.
7 **A** How long time have you been learning English? _____
  B For about three years.
8 **A** Whose jacket did you borrow for the wedding? _____
  B My dad's. It was a little big for me.
9 **A** Excuse me. Can you tell me where is the bathroom? _____
  B It's down the stairs on the right.
10 **A** For who are you waiting? _____
  B I'm waiting for my brother.

b Write indirect questions.

1 "Where does Natalie live?"
  I wonder _where Natalie lives_.
2 "Where is the elevator?"
  Could you tell me _____?
3 "Where did we park the car?"
  I can't remember _____.
4 "Are there any tickets left for the concert tonight?"
  Do you know _____?
5 "What time does the game start?"
  Can you tell me _____?
6 "When's Anna's birthday?"
  Can you remember _____?

c Write the questions.

1 when / your brother / pass / his driver's test
  When did your brother pass his driver's test?

2 who / cook / in your family
  _____?

3 how long / you / spend / in Brazil last summer
  _____?

4 you know / who / go / to the party tonight
  _____?

5 you remember / where / I / leave / my keys
  _____?

6 what / make / you angry
  _____?

7 who / drink / the milk / I / leave / in the refrigerator
  _____?

8 how long / it / take / to get to Boston from here
  _____?

2 READING & VOCABULARY

a Read the article quickly and match the titles to the paragraphs.

A **Criticizing past employers**
B **Talking too much**
C **Doubts about your résumé**
D **Bringing a drink with you**
E **Ignorance of the company**

b Look at the highlighted words and phrases in the text and try to figure out their meaning. Then match them to definitions 1–10.

1 that cannot be forgiven _____
2 connected with what is being discussed _____
3 making you very nervous or worried _____-_____
4 stupid mistakes _____
5 be unable to answer a question _____
6 from memory _____
7 start talking about something less important
_____ _____-_____
8 drinking a very small amount of liquid at a time _____
9 dislike very much _____
10 play with something because you are nervous _____

Most common interview mistakes

A job interview is a nerve-racking experience at the best of times, so it's important to prepare for it well. Arriving late is sure to ruin your chances, as is dressing inappropriately. And do not dream of answering your phone during the interview. Read on for five more common blunders and how to avoid making them.

1 _____ This is a highly unprofessional habit, as it suggests a serious inability to manage your time. Surely you could have planned your schedule better to include a coffee stop beforehand? Having a cup in your hand creates the opportunity for distraction: you might fiddle with it or miss a question while taking a sip of coffee. Worse still, its contents may end up on the desk, which will result in the interviewer remembering you for all the wrong reasons.

2 _____ In this age of technology, it is inexcusable not to know anything about your prospective employer. Most company websites these days have an "About Us" section giving company history, locations, divisions, and a mission statement. Do some research before the Big Day and you won't be stumped if the interviewer asks you a question about the place where you, theoretically, want to work.

3 _____ An interview is a professional situation, not a personal one, so the interviewer will not want to hear your life story. While you need to answer all the questions you are asked, your responses should be focused and to the point. Don't get side-tracked and talk about your home life, your partner, and any children you may have – save this for the first day on your new job when you are getting to know your colleagues.

4 _____ It is important to maintain a positive attitude throughout the interview, even when discussing things that have gone wrong. Don't let the interviewer know that you want to leave your current job because you can't stand your boss. Saying unpleasant things about your colleagues is not a good idea, because the interviewer might know them. Also, you will be showing him how you will speak about his company if you leave on bad terms in the future.

5 _____ Not being familiar with your past history of employment creates a very bad impression. It suggests that either you have a very bad memory, or you made up some of the facts. Make sure you know the basic information by heart because the interviewer is sure to ask you about it. If you really do have a bad memory, take a copy to refer to, but do not appear to be reading it out loud.

3 PRONUNCIATION friendly intonation

a `ONLINE` Listen and complete the questions.

1 *What kind of music* _____ do you like to listen to?
2 _____ did you go to?
3 _____ in an office?
4 _____ for the future?
5 _____ abroad?
6 _____ do you speak?

b Listen and repeat. Copy the rhythm.

4 LISTENING

a `ONLINE` Read the job ad and listen to an interview for the job. Is the applicant successful or unsuccessful?

Complete**Jobs**

CURRENT VACANCIES

Employer:	Park Hotel, New York City
Job:	Receptionist
Contract:	Temporary
Hours:	Full-Time
Salary:	$2,200 per month

b Listen again and look at the list of common interview mistakes. Circle the mistake that the applicant makes.

1 bringing a drink
2 talking too much
3 criticizing past employers
4 ignorance of the company
5 doubts about his résumé

c Listen again and complete the sentences.

1 Stephen Bridges went to the interview by _____ and _____.
2 He wants a temporary job because he's moving across the country in _____.
3 Stephen has a degree in _____.
4 He worked in a _____ for _____.
5 He can speak _____ foreign languages.
6 Most of the Asian guests come from _____.
7 In his previous job, Stephen didn't have to _____.
8 Stephen thinks he has the _____ for the job.

d Listen again with the audio script on p.69 and try to guess the meaning of any words you don't know. Then check in your dictionary.

USEFUL WORDS AND PHRASES

Learn these words and phrases.

approach (n) /əˈproʊtʃ/
bizarre /bɪˈzɑr/
job candidate /dʒoʊb ˈkændədeɪt/
crush (somebody or something) /krʌʃ/
demanding /dɪˈmændɪŋ/
flustered (adj) /ˈflʌstərd/
job seekers /dʒoʊb ˈsikərz/
rather than /ˈræðər ðæn/
recruitment agency /rɪˈkrutmənt ˈeɪdʒənsi/
think on your feet /θɪŋk ɑn yɔr fit/

Here's something to think about:
How come you never see a headline like "Psychic Wins Lottery"?

Jay Leno, American comedian & television host

1B Do you believe in it?

1 READING

a Read the text. Which topic is <u>not</u> mentioned?

politics relationships business food sports

The dream destination for astrology addicts

While in the US the general belief in astrology is limited to glancing at horoscopes in newspapers and magazines, in India people take their star signs very seriously indeed.

Astrology programs are shown on many of India's 320 television channels, and at least a dozen stations are devoted entirely to astrology 24 hours a day. Kolkata housewife Lata Banerji always starts her day by turning on the astrology channel, Shristi, to find out what the day holds for her and whether she will have to face any kind of domestic crisis. She also receives information on what food she should eat to avoid illness. "It gives me the confidence I need to face the day," she says. "Americans go to a therapist every week to cope with life. I get my sense of well-being from the advice I get from astrologers."

Astrology is important in India in all walks of life, but especially when it comes to choosing a marriage partner. Some astrological combinations are considered unfavorable, for example when the planet Mars is in a certain position on a person's birth

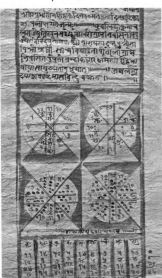

chart. In this case, people believe that the couple will not get along and that their marriage will end badly. The only way around this is for the person with the unlucky combination to "marry" something symbolic before their real wedding. This is exactly what Bollywood actress and former Miss World, Aishwarya Rai did some years ago when she "married" a banana tree in the hope of avoiding problems in her marriage with the actor Abhishek Bachchan.

Yet, it is not only in the field of love that Indians seek astrological advice. There are

b Read the text again and choose the right answer.

1 …radio stations are only about astrology.
  a 320   b 12   c 24
2 Lata Banerji watches an astrology channel…
  a to help her in her daily life.
  b because she is very worried about getting sick.
  c because she can't afford a therapist.
3 The actress Aishwarya Rai married a tree…
  a to make sure it produced a lot of bananas.
  b to bring her luck in the search for a husband.
  c to ensure her marriage was successful.
4 According to the text, Indians ask astrologers…
  a how they should vote in the election.
  b where they can get a good job.
  c for advice about many things.
5 Sunita Menon works as…
  a an adviser for a well-known company.
  b a tarot card reader.
  c a flight attendant.

c Look at the highlighted words and phrases. What do you think they mean? Use your dictionary to look up their meaning and pronunciation.

some programs on TV that specialize in medical astrology, with callers asking about health issues. Others provide investment and business advice. Astrology is even important in politics with prime ministers asking their astrologers for a "promising" date before announcing a general election.

Nowadays it is almost obligatory for Indian parents to have a horoscope drawn up when a baby is born. Two people taking advantage of the boom in business are Kalidas Sriram and Vishi Babu, who have put up their tents complete with laptop computer and printer, right outside Kolkata's main hospital. They either visit the maternity wards or wait outside until new parents leave to offer their services. For the equivalent of $4, they use the baby's time and date of birth to print out a horoscope for the happy parents.

Many Indians have no doubt that astrology can change people's lives for the better. The glamorous Sunita Menon, India's most famous fortune-teller, was an air hostess until a tarot reader predicted that she would change jobs. Now she is the host of a hugely popular television program and was recently hired by India's most famous music company to give advice about investment and business decisions.

Sunita Menon

2 VOCABULARY compound adjectives

Complete the sentences with compound adjectives formed from the words in parentheses.

1 My grandmother is always forgetting her keys. She's very _absentminded_ . (mind)

2 Oliver's wife isn't as crazy as he is. She seems very _____. (balance)

3 Our English teacher doesn't get angry easily. She's extremely _____. (temper)

4 My parents are very _____. They won't listen to other people's opinions. (mind)

5 Grace never thinks of anyone else because she's so _____. (center)

6 My sister-in-law is very _____. She says one thing and does another. (face)

7 Since he went abroad, Jack has become more _____ about other cultures. (mind)

8 You won't be able to change her mind – she's very _____. (will)

9 When we go out, my friend Jack never offers to pay for gas. I wish he wasn't so _____. (fist)

10 The new manager thinks a lot of himself. He's very _____. (head)

3 MINI GRAMMAR *the... the...* + comparatives

Complete the sentences with the correct form of the words in parentheses.

1 The _more you worry_ about it, the _worse_ you'll feel. (worry a lot, bad)

2 The _____ you own, the _____ you become. (a lot of gadgets, lazy)

3 The _____ you are, the _____ he'll be. (late, angry)

4 The _____ my English, the _____ I'll speak. (practice a lot, good)

5 The _____ it gets, the _____ you have to wear. (cold, a lot of clothes)

6 The _____ you do, the _____ you'll get. (a lot of exercise, strong)

4 GRAMMAR auxiliary verbs

Complete the dialogues with a tag question or an auxiliary and the subject if necessary.

1 **A** I texted you last night, but you didn't reply.
  B Yes, _I did_ reply. I texted you right away.

2 **A** I don't feel like cooking tonight.
  B Neither _____. Let's go out for dinner. I'd love some Mexican food.
  A So _____. Come on. Let's go.

3 **A** I've seen this movie before.
  B Well, I _____.
  A Do you mind if I change channels?
  B Yes, I _____ mind! I want to see the end.

4 **A** You are going to Sam's party, _____?
  B No, I'm not.
  A Why not? You haven't argued with him again, _____?
  B Yes. And we aren't going out anymore.

5 **A** I'll be back a little bit late tonight.
  B You _____ ? Where are you going?
  A To a concert with some friends.
  B Oh, OK. You'll be back before 12, _____?
  A Of course.

6 **A** Pete, you couldn't lend me some money _____?
  B No, sorry. Why?
  A I spent my entire salary already this month.
  B So _____. That's why I can't lend you any!

7 **A** I didn't go out last night.
  B Neither _____. I was too tired.
  A So _____.

8 **A** You aren't from around here, _____?
  B No, I'm from Australia. I haven't been here long.
  A I don't suppose you like this cold weather.
  B Actually, I _____ like it. I prefer cool weather to hot weather.

5 PRONUNCIATION intonation and sentence rhythm

ONLINE Listen and repeat the conversations. <u>Copy</u> the <u>rhythm</u>, stressing the bold auxiliaries.

1 A You **don't** like the soup, **do** you?
  B I **do** like it. It's just that it's very hot.

2 A You **haven't** bought me a present, **have** you?
  B I **have** bought you one. It's just that I left it at home.

3 A You **aren't** enjoying this movie, **are** you?
  B I **am** enjoying it. It's just that I've seen it before.

4 A You **didn't** bring any money, **did** you?
  B I **did** bring some money. It's just that I spent it all.

5 A You **won't** ever wear those pants I gave you, **will** you?
  B I **will** wear them. It's just that I prefer wearing jeans.

6 A You **can't** play tennis, **can** you?
  B I **can** play tennis. It's just that I'm not very good at it.

6 LISTENING

a **ONLINE** Listen to a radio program about superstitions and complete the chart.

Superstition	When or where?	Why?
	Originated in the Middle [1]_____	People thought black cats possessed evil [2]_____
	Originated in ancient [3]_____	People thought it broke the [4]_____ of the triangle
	Originated in the [5]_____	People knocked on [6]_____ to call the good spirits
	Originated at the time of the [7]_____	The Pope passed a law obliging people to bless the person who was [8]_____

b Listen again with the audio script on p.69 and try to guess the meaning of any words that you don't know. Then check in your dictionary.

USEFUL WORDS AND PHRASES

Learn these words and phrases.

binoculars /bɪˈnɑkyələrz/
breeze /briz/
continue (doing something) /kənˈtɪnyu/
curtains /ˈkərtnz/
dome /doʊm/

drag (something across the floor) /dræg/
real estate agent /ril ɪˈsteɪt eɪdʒənt/
glide /glaɪd/
hallucinate /həˈlusəneɪt/
row houses /ˈroʊ ˈhaʊzəz/

Colloquial English Talking about... interviews

1 LOOKING AT LANGUAGE

Match the formal words in sentences 1–10 with the informal words in the box.

answer begin buy check end fill out ~~follow~~ say see show

1 My colleague was dismissed because she didn't **adhere to** the terms of her contract. _follow_

2 Please **state** your preference for a telephone or face-to-face interview. _____

3 The next training course will **commence** on June 1st. _____

4 The receptionist asked me to **complete** an application form. _____

5 These figures **demonstrate** the problems facing the company. _____

6 Customers are advised to retain their receipt when they **purchase** an item. _____

7 The candidate made no **response** when he was asked about his experience. _____

8 My contract will **terminate** at the end of the year. _____

9 They called the candidate's work references to **verify** his work history. _____

10 We **view** your prospects of promotion as very high. _____

2 READING

a Read the article. Mark the sentences **T** (true) or **F** (false).

1 Guy Goma was invited to the BBC because he had applied for a job. ____

2 Mr. Goma was hoping to be taken on as a cleaner. ____

3 Mr. Goma was interviewed as soon as he arrived. ____

4 IT expert, Guy Kewney, was at the BBC at the same time as Guy Goma. ____

5 Guy Kewney had been invited to appear on a news show. ____

6 Both men were waiting at the same reception area. ____

7 The producer collected the wrong man for the news show. ____

8 Mr. Goma became aware of the mistake while he was being prepared for the interview. ____

9 Mr. Goma admitted that he wasn't Mr. Kewney on live television. ____

10 In the end, Mr. Goma was not offered a job at the BBC. ____

b Look at the highlighted words and phrases. What do you think they mean? Use your dictionary to look up their meaning and pronunciation.

The wrong man for the job!

Mix up at BBC leads to job applicant appearing on live TV.

All sorts of things can go wrong in a job interview, ranging from spilling a drink to your cell phone ringing – the list is endless. Few applicants, however, turn up for their interview and end up appearing live on television. This is exactly what happened to 43-year-old Guy Goma when he went to a job interview at the BBC.

Mr. Goma, from the Republic of the Congo, had applied for the position of data support cleanser, a job that involves updating records on a database. On the day of the interview, he arrived at BBC Television Center in plenty of time and was told to wait in the main reception area until he was called.

At the same time, News 24 host Karen Bowerman was preparing to interview British technology expert Guy Kewney about the verdict of the Apple versus Apple court case. This was a high-profile case between Apple Computer and The Beatles' record label Apple Corps over the rights to use the name "Apple." Mr. Kewney was waiting for his TV appearance in another reception area. The mix-up occurred when a producer went to get the technology expert from the wrong reception area.

The producer approached Mr. Goma and asked him if he was Guy. Hearing his first name, Mr. Goma said that he was and he was taken to the News 24 studio. After having makeup put on, he was seated in front of the cameras and wired with a microphone. Although Mr. Goma thought all the preparations very unusual, he prepared to do his best for what he believed would be his job interview.

A few moments later, Ms. Bowerman introduced Mr. Goma on live television as technology expert Guy Kewney. At first, Mr. Goma became visibly shocked, but then he simply played along because he did not want to make a scene. He did his best to answer three questions about the verdict of the court case and its implications for the music industry. Meanwhile, Mr. Kewney, still in the waiting area and looking up at a TV screen, was astonished to see Mr. Goma being interviewed in his place.

As soon as the mistake was realized, the BBC recorded an interview with Mr. Kewney for later broadcast, but it was never shown. Twenty minutes after appearing live on TV, Mr. Goma attended his real job interview, which lasted for just ten minutes, but he did not get the job. A spokesperson for the BBC said that they were looking carefully at their guest procedures and that they would take every measure to ensure that the misunderstanding didn't happen again. Mr. Goma became a minor celebrity for a while, and he appeared on several TV shows.

2A Call the doctor?

1 READING

a Read the article. Complete it with the missing sentences. There is one sentence you don't need to use.

A Making an effort to focus on the page means that we blink less often.

B Each of its functions happens in a particular area, and different regions are used for different tasks.

C This is because the flow of blood to the brain decreases while the body digests it.

D Furthermore, existing studies suggest that adequate fluid intake is usually met through our daily consumption of juice, milk, and caffeinated drinks.

E When the dead part above the surface of the skin is removed, the living section underneath is not affected.

b Read the text again. Mark the sentences **T** (true) or **F** (false).

1 Doctors spend a lot of time investigating myths.   *F*

2 At the beginning of the 1900s, people believed that we only used a small part of our brains.   ___

3 Unshaven hair is exactly the same color as hair under the surface of the skin.   ___

4 In the past, people's eyesight was worse because they read by candlelight.   ___

5 Turkey contains less tryptophan than cheese.   ___

c Look at the highlighted words and phrases. What do you think they mean? Use your dictionary to look up their meaning and pronunciation.

Medical myths

Good doctors are always learning new things, but very few of them question existing medical myths. A well-known medical journal recently examined the most common of these to see if there is any evidence that they are true. This is what they discovered.

Myth: We only use about 10% of our brains

This myth appeared in the early twentieth century, when the concept of self-improvement was born. The idea was that there are many abilities built into our brains, but if we do not develop them, we never learn how to do them. This led to the belief that there are parts of our brains that we do not use. However, scientific evidence shows that this is not the case. Brain scans have revealed that there is no area of the brain that is silent or inactive. [1]_____ Nobody who has examined the brain has been able to identify the 90% that we, supposedly, do not use.

Myth: Shaving hair causes it to grow back thicker

This belief is often reinforced by the media, despite the fact that a clinical trial in 1928 showed that shaving has no effect on hair growth. [2]_____ This makes it unlikely for the hair to grow back any different than it was before. The reason it appears thicker is that recently shaved hair lacks the finer point seen at the ends of unshaven hair. In addition to this, the new hair has not been lightened by the sun, which makes it look darker than the hair that has already grown.

Myth: Reading in insufficient light ruins your eyesight

People tend to believe this because of the discomfort they experience when they have been reading for a while in dim light. [3]_____ This causes our eyes to dry out and feel uncomfortable. Fortunately, the effect is only temporary and most ophthalmologists* agree that it doesn't damage our eyes permanently. Something else that disproves the myth is that there are more short-sighted people today than in the past, when reading conditions were worse. Before the invention of electricity, people relied on candles or lanterns to read, yet fewer people needed glasses.

*ophthalmologists – doctors who specialize in eyes

Myth: Eating turkey makes people feel especially tired

Some foods contain a natural chemical called tryptophan, which is known to cause drowsiness. The myth is the idea that consuming turkey (and the tryptophan it contains) might make someone more likely to fall asleep. Actually, both chicken and ground beef have nearly the same amount of tryptophan as turkey; other foods, such as pork or cheese, contain even more. The truth is that any large, solid meal can make you feel sleepy, whether it contains turkey or not. [4]_____ It isn't the turkey in your dinner that puts you to sleep; it is the quantity of food that you have eaten.

2 VOCABULARY illness and treatment

a Complete the sentences with a verb from the box.

be sick   burn   choke   ~~cough~~   cut   faint   hurt   sneeze

1 The smoke from the fire made everybody ___cough___.
2 I'm feeling a little dizzy. I think I'm going to _____.
3 I'm allergic to cats. They make me _____.
4 Be careful! You'll _____ your back if you try to lift that heavy chair by yourself.
5 That knife is very sharp. Please don't _____ yourself.
6 I'm not feeling well. I think I'm going to _____.
7 Be careful! You might _____ yourself. The oven's really hot.
8 Some people don't like eating fish because they're worried that they'll _____ on the fish bones.

b Complete the dialogues between the **p**atients and the **d**octor.

1 **P** I have a temperature and my body aches.
  D I think you have the _flu_.
2 **P** I'm tired and I don't have any energy.
  D It sounds like you have low bl_____ pr_____.
3 **P** There's a rash all over my body.
  D You probably had an a_____ r_____ to something.
4 **P** I hurt my wrist playing tennis and it's very swollen.
  D You might have spr_____ it.
5 **P** It hurts when I talk and when I eat.
  D You have a s_____ thr_____.
6 **P** I'm really sick and I have diarrhea.
  D I think you have f_____ p_____.

c Complete the crossword.

Clues across →

1 If you sprain your ankle, the best thing is to put ice on it and do this to it.
5 You can take these tablets for an allergy.
6 You can put this kind of antibiotic product on a small cut on your finger.

Clues down ↓

2 The doctor will give you these if you have an infection.
3 You can take these when you have a headache.
4 If you have a deep cut, you will probably need these to close the wound.

3 GRAMMAR
present perfect simple and continuous

a <u>Underline</u> the correct form.

1 How long *are your parents* | <u>*have your parents been*</u> married?
2 Nathan got the job, but he *hasn't yet started* | *hasn't started yet*.
3 *Have you had ever* | *Have you ever had* an operation?
4 I can't go out now because *I just washed* | *I washed just* my hair.
5 Kate has had a cold *for* | *since* last weekend.
6 We've had this computer *for* | *since* two months.
7 My son *is* | *has been* late for school three times so far this week.
8 They *only know* | *have only known* each other for a week, but they're already good friends.

b Complete the email with the correct form of the verbs in parentheses. Use the present perfect simple or continuous.

Dear Teresa,

Sorry I [1] *haven't written* (not write) for a while, but I [2]_____ (have) a lot of work recently, and I [3]_____ (be) too exhausted to do anything in the evenings once I get home. Today is a holiday though, so I [4]_____ (write) emails all day to try to catch up with all my friends.

Guess what! I [5]_____ (move out) of my parents' house! I [6]_____ (live) in my new apartment for a week now, and I love it! I [7]_____ (already / unpack) all my things and it's beginning to feel like home. You have to come and visit!

The bad news is that I [8]_____ (break up) with Andrew. He [9]_____ (travel) so much recently that we [10]_____ (not manage) to see each other much, and I [11]_____ (meet) someone else. His name is Carl and he's a colleague from work. We [12]_____ (see) each other since the beginning of the summer. We [13]_____ (have) three dates so far and I really like him!

Anyway, got to go. Please write soon and tell me all your news.
Love,
Sophie

4 PRONUNCIATION

/ʃ/, /k/, /dʒ/ and /tʃ/; word stress

a (Circle) the word with a different sound.

1 ʃ shower	pre**ss**ure ra**sh** infe**ct**ion (**ch**est)	
2 k keys	a**ch**e si**ck** spe**ci**alist **ch**olesterol	
3 dʒ jazz	aller**g**ic fin**g**er emer**g**ency in**j**ury	
4 tʃ chess	**ch**oke tempera**t**ure sti**tch**es stoma**ch**	
5 ʃ shower	cou**ch** con**sci**ousness opera**t**ion **sh**ock	
6 dʒ jazz	banda**g**e in**j**ection ne**g**ative sur**g**ery	

b ONLINE Listen and check. Then listen and repeat the words.

c Underline the stress in the words.

1 an|ti|bi|o|tic
2 a|ller|gic
3 di|a|rrhe|a
4 di|zzy
5 head|ache
6 me|di|cine
7 swo|llen
8 tem|pera|ture
9 vo|mit
10 un|con|scious

d ONLINE Listen and check. Then listen and repeat the words.

5 LISTENING

a ONLINE Listen and complete the **Emergency** column of the table.

	What was the emergency?	What was the treatment?
Speaker 1	*a serious cut on the head*	_____
Speaker 2	_____	_____
Speaker 3	_____	_____
Speaker 4	_____	_____
Speaker 5	_____	_____

b Listen again and complete the **Treatment** column of the table.

c Listen again with the audio script on p.70 and try to guess the meaning of any words that you don't know. Then check in your dictionary.

USEFUL WORDS AND PHRASES

Learn these words and phrases.

alternative remedies /ɔl'tərnətɪv 'rɛmədiz/
brain (tumor) /breɪn/
chest infection /tʃɛst ɪn'fɛkʃn/
heart rate /hɑrt reɪt/
hypochondriac /haɪpə'kɑndriæk/
life-threatening illness /laɪf 'θrɛtnɪŋ 'ɪlnəs/
open heart surgery /oʊpən hɑrt 'sərdʒəri/
pulse /pʌls/
(mouth) ulcer /'ʌlsər/
under the weather /'ʌndər ðə 'wɛðər/

If you can speak three languages, you are trilingual. If you can speak two, you are bilingual. If you can speak only one, you are American.

Author unknown

2B Older and wiser?

1 GRAMMAR adjectives as nouns, adjective order

a Complete the sentences with *the* + adjective.

1 **China** *The Chinese* won the most gold medals at the 2012 Olympics.
2 **Japan** _____ eat a lot of fish.
3 **Vietnam** _____ usually celebrate Tet in January or February.
4 **Switzerland** _____ have a good standard of living.

5 **Portugal** _____ are very kind and friendly to visitors.
6 **England** _____ have a reputation for being polite.
7 **Scotland** _____ enjoy spending time outdoors.

8 **France** _____ are extremely fond of bike riding.

b Complete the sentences with the noun form of an adjective from the box.

| blind | ~~deaf~~ | disabled | injured | elderly | rich | unemployed | young |

1 *The deaf* usually communicate with each other using sign language.
2 The government is offering courses to help _____ to find jobs.
3 After the accident, _____ were taken to the hospital.
4 The building has easy access for _____.
5 Do you think _____ should pay higher taxes than the poor?
6 In some countries, _____ use special dogs to help them find their way around.
7 _____ always think that they know better than their parents.
8 Should the family or the state take care of _____?

c Right (✓) or wrong (✗)? Correct the mistakes in the highlighted phrases.

1 Sarah's wearing a denim short skirt.
  ✗ *a short denim skirt*
2 I'm looking for a sleeveless cotton T-shirt.
  _____
3 I want to buy some leather white pants.
  _____
4 My sister's bought some purple trendy glasses.
  _____
5 He gave his mother a patterned silk scarf for her birthday.
  _____
6 He looks very fashionable in his gray new Armani suit.
  _____
7 She was wearing a bright red wool scarf.
  _____
8 You can't wear those old scruffy jeans to the wedding.
  _____

2 READING

a Read the article quickly. Check (✓) the sentences that are right and put an (✗) on the ones that are wrong.

Hipsters…
1 always look fashionable. ____
2 go shopping as often as they can. ____
3 care a lot about current affairs. ____
4 love listening to music. ____
5 eat in fast food restaurants. ____

How to be a **Hipster**

Today, hipsters can be seen more frequently than ever before. They are part of a subculture that rejects everything mainstream in favor of expressing their own uniqueness. If this sort of thing appeals to you, you might like to consider becoming a hipster yourself. Read on to find out more.

1 Dress like a hipster

Hipsters would never wear designer clothes because they prefer to create their own image. Indispensable items in a hipster's wardrobe include skinny jeans or leggings and T-shirts with ironic messages printed on them. Plaid and flower patterns are also popular, and it doesn't matter if the garments don't match. They wear cowboy boots or Converse sneakers on their feet, and as far as accessories are concerned, they wear sunglasses, bright belts, and they generally have a couple of piercings.

2 Shopping

Consumerism is something that hipsters can't stand, so they don't go shopping very often. Instead they prefer to make use of old things, and they love vintage clothing. Female hipsters raid their grandmothers' closets looking for old dresses, while the men go in search of Grandpa's old shirts – the ones without a collar. Of course, the clothes generally need to be altered to make them fit, but a hipster is a genius with a needle and thread, so this isn't a problem. The only stores a hipster will enter are thrift shops, craft stores, or their local vintage boutique.

3 Lifestyle

Hipsters tend to be very bothered and upset about the way the world works – or doesn't work, in their view. They are usually well-informed because they spend hours every day sitting in cafés surfing the Internet on their smartphones or tablets – the only exceptions to their aversion to consumerism. Hipsters are usually young – the age ranges from late teens to mid-30s. Most go to college, and many of them base their career choices around music, art, or fashion.

4 Entertainment

Hipsters love all things independent and Indie music is a big part of what they represent. They are always the first to hear about new bands, but once a band becomes popular, they stop listening to it. A typical hipster line is: "I liked them before they were cool." When it comes to movies, they watch independent and foreign films, and they attend independent productions at the theater. Hipsters also love reading, especially books about political science, anthropology, and sociology.

5 Food

Eating meat isn't popular with hipsters, and most of them tend to be vegetarians or vegans. Many grow their own food in their gardens or on a balcony; if not, they go to natural food markets instead. Fruit, coffee, and Asian food are very popular with hipsters, and they love making meals for their foodie friends.

So if you want to be a hipster, forget everything you know about being "cool" and find your own unique way to fit in with this trend.

b Read the article again and choose the right answer.

1 The hipster subculture is made up of people who want…
   a to look cool.
   b to be different.
   c to fit in.

2 Hipsters don't tend to wear…
   a sports shoes.
   b colorful patterns.
   c baggy pants.

3 Hipsters sometimes go shopping in…
   a stores that support a good cause.
   b stores that sell the latest fashions.
   c places that everyone knows.

4 Many hipsters…
   a like to read about politics.
   b are involved in politics.
   c know very little about politics.

5 Hipsters like new music…
   a after it has become well known.
   b until it becomes well known.
   c when others stop liking it.

6 Hipsters enjoy food…
   a from supermarkets.
   b they produce themselves.
   c in restaurants.

c Find the words or phrases in the text to match definitions 1–10:

1 adjective referring to ideas and opinions thought to be normal because they are shared by most people *(introduction)*
   _____

2 the general impression that a person gives *(paragraph 1)* _____

3 things that you wear or carry to match your clothes, e.g., bag, scarf *(paragraph 1)*
   _____

4 garments from a certain period in the past *(paragraph 2)* _____ _____

5 things you use for sewing *(paragraph 2)*
   _____ _____

6 worried about something *(paragraph 3)*
   _____

7 a strong feeling of not liking something *(paragraph 3)* _____

8 not influenced by anything else *(paragraph 4)*
   _____

9 people who don't eat any animal products at all *(paragraph 5)*
   _____

10 a person who is very interested in trying different dishes *(paragraph 5)*
   _____

3 VOCABULARY clothes and fashion

a Order the letters in the parentheses to make a material. Then complete the sentences.

1 Jack was wearing a blue _denim_ jacket. (NEDIM)
2 I prefer to wear light _____ shirts in the summer. (TCONTO)
3 I gave my mom a blouse with a _____ collar for her birthday. (ALCE)
4 Are you sure those boots are made of _____? (EHATELR)
5 I never buy _____ clothes because they take so long to iron. (ENNIL)
6 They gave me a very expensive _____ tie as a going-away present. (LIKS)
7 Don't wear your _____ jacket out – it's raining. (DESEU)
8 I really like your new _____ jacket. Where did you get it? (ETLEVV)

b Circle the odd one that doesn't belong.

1 hooded   sleeveless   (tight)   V-neck
2 long-sleeved   old-fashioned   stylish   trendy
3 plaid   silk   dotted   striped
4 denim   fur   loose   suede
5 fashionable   patterned   scruffy   tight

c Complete the sentences with a verb from the box.

dress up	fit	get changed	get undressed
go with	hang up	~~match~~	suits

1 That shirt doesn't _match_ your jacket. It doesn't look right.
2 The party's going to be very formal, so I guess we'd better _____ .
3 Can you _____ your shirts in the closet, please? I just ironed them.
4 I think I must have gained some weight. These pants don't _____ me anymore.
5 You look great in that new dress! It really _____ you.
6 I've been working in the yard, so I'll have to _____ before we go out.
7 Gina is looking for a top to _____ her new pants.
8 Can you tell the children to _____ and jump into the bathtub, please?

4 PRONUNCIATION vowel sounds

a Circle the word with a different sound.

1 ![boot] boot	2 ![bull] bull	3 ![fish] fish	4 ![bird] bird	5 ![tree] tree	6 ![egg] egg
loose	cotton	linen	fur	jeans	V-neck
(scruffy)	hooded	slippers	shirt	sleeveless	cheap
shoes	put	silk	shorts	leather	denim
suit	wool	striped	skirt	green	trendy

b ONLINE Listen and check. Then listen and repeat.

5 LISTENING

a ONLINE Listen to a radio program about aging. Is Laura, the guest on the program, optimistic or pessimistic about getting old?

b Listen again and mark the sentences **T** (true) or **F** (false).

1 The elderly tend to be miserable. ___
2 Our future health is programmed entirely by our genes. ___
3 Some people lead busy lives when they reach old age. ___
4 The increase in the number of old people contributes to overpopulation. ___
5 The elderly will be lonely in the future. ___

c Listen again with the audio script on p.70 and try to guess the meaning of any words that you don't know. Then check in your dictionary.

USEFUL WORDS AND PHRASES

Learn these words and phrases.

break down (and cry) /breɪk daʊn/
deal with /dil wɪð/
elderly /ˈɛldərli/
makeup (n) /ˈmeɪkʌp/
treat (v) /trit/
trick (sb) /trɪk/
vulnerable /ˈvʌlnərəbl/
wig /wɪg/
wise /waɪz/
wrinkles /ˈrɪŋklz/

ONLINE FILE 2

3A The truth about air travel

1 READING

a Read the text once. What did the four incidents have in common?

   A They all happened before the plane took off.
   B They all happened during the flight.
   C They all happened during the summer.
   D None of the above.

b Read the text again and complete it with the missing sentences. There is one sentence you do not have to use.

   A Unfortunately, they did this incredibly slowly, and no planes could take off until they had completed their journey.

   B Somehow, the animals managed to open the box and jump out of the hold of the plane onto the runway.

   C The pilot spoke to the passengers, who were very angry, to try to calm them down.

   D The cancellation announcement was made when the 169 passengers were waiting to board at the gate.

   E However, there was thick fog at the time, and so the flight was diverted to Liege in Belgium, about 180 miles away.

c Look at the highlighted words and phrases in the text and try to figure out their meaning. Then match them to definitions 1–7.

   1 arrive _____

   2 the part of an aircraft where goods are stored
   _____

   3 something that you can choose to do
   _____

   4 incidents that make it difficult for something to continue in the usual way
   _____

   5 arranged to be done at a particular time
   _____

   6 a period of time worked by a group of workers who start work as another group finishes
   _____

   7 get off an aircraft _____

Why are we waiting?

The usual excuses for flight delays are bad weather, strikes, or technical faults, but sometimes problems are caused by more unexpected events. Below are some of the most unusual reasons for flight disruptions at the world's airports.

Where's the pilot?

In November 2011, an Air India flight had to be canceled in southern India because there was no one to fly the plane. [1]____ The pilot who was supposed to fly the plane refused to do so because he had already completed his shift. The airline called someone to substitute for him, but the second pilot did not turn up. In the end, half of the passengers took a different Air India flight and the rest had to travel on a different airline.

Love is in the air

Last year, services were disrupted at New York's JFK Airport by a group of lovesick turtles. It seems that the turtles wanted to get from the area where they had been feeding to their breeding grounds, so they had no other option but to cross the runway. [2]____ Airport authorities say that this is not the first time that flights have been delayed by the turtles, but they can never predict exactly when the crossing will take place.

Passenger protest

In November 2010, Ryanair's flight schedule was interrupted by a protest by the people on board. Most of them were French tourists who had been on vacation in Morocco. The flight had already been delayed for three hours before it left Fez, Morocco, and so everyone was looking forward to arriving at Paris's Beauvais Airport. [3]____ When the plane landed, about 100 passengers demanded to be flown to Paris and refused to disembark. About four hours later, they were finally persuaded to leave the plane and board the buses that would take them to Paris.

The great escape

In December 2009, a Continental Airlines flight was delayed in Houston, in the US, because two animals had gotten out of their box in the hold. The animals were sea otters, a marine mammal with dense fur that lives in the northern and eastern parts of the Pacific Ocean. [4]____ Passengers had to wait 80 minutes for the sea otters to be caught before their plane could take off. Their flight was scheduled to leave for Columbus, Ohio, at 7:55 p.m., but they did not take off until 9:15 p.m.

2 VOCABULARY air travel

a Complete the crossword.

Crossword with:
1 c
2 u
  s
  t
3
4 o
  m
  s
5
6
7
8

1 All of the passengers on our flight were stopped at… for their bags to be checked.
2 We could see our plane on the…while we were waiting to board.
3 After we'd checked in, we went through to…to find the right gate.
4 Despite the rain, my plane took off…, exactly as scheduled.
5 My first flight was…for two hours, so I missed my connecting flight.
6 Our suitcases were really heavy, so we went to find a… to put them on.
7 When I got to the airport, I went straight to…to see if my mother's flight had landed yet.
8 The cabin…was very efficient when we had to make an emergency landing.

b Complete the text with suitable words.

The worst trip I ever took was when I flew to New York last year. I arrived at the ¹terminal in plenty of time, but when I got to the ²ch_____-_____ desk, there was a huge line. By the time it was my turn, there were no ³a_____ seats left, so I had to sit in the middle of a row. I showed my ID card to the man at passport control and then I went to ⁴s_____ where I had my scissors confiscated. My ⁵fl_____ was already boarding as soon as I arrived at the departure lounge, and I had to run to reach the gate in time. I sat next to a small child who screamed loudly when we ⁶t_____ _____, and didn't stop screaming for the next two hours. The weather over the Atlantic was terrible and we experienced a lot of ⁷t_____. I was so relieved when we finally landed in New York. The worst thing was that when I went to baggage claim to ⁸p_____ _____ my baggage, I was told that my suitcase hadn't arrived. I spent my first two days in New York with no clothes!

3 MINI GRAMMAR so / such…that

Circle the correct answer.

1 Her suitcase was (so)/ such heavy that she couldn't pick it up.

2 I've never had such / such a bumpy flight – there was a lot of turbulence.

3 This is the first time we've had a so long / such a long delay at the airport.

4 The terminal was so / such crowded that we couldn't find a cart for our suitcases.

5 There was so much / so many traffic that we almost missed our flight.

6 There were so / such a lot of people at the airport because it was a holiday weekend.

4 GRAMMAR past perfect continuous, narrative tenses

a Circle the correct verb form. Check (✓) if both are correct.

1 Tim's suitcase was really heavy because he (had packed)/ had been packing all of his camera equipment.
2 Jessica was fed up because she *had waited | had been waiting* for three hours for her flight to board.
3 I *had been sitting | had sat* in departures for 20 minutes when I realized my flight was already boarding.
4 After I *had picked up | had been picking up* my baggage, I took a taxi to my hotel.
5 The kids were bored because we *had stood | had been standing* in line at check-in for over an hour.
6 My flight arrived late because it *hadn't taken off | hadn't been taking off* on time.

b Complete the text with the correct form of the verb in parentheses.

My parents [1] _had never flown_ (never fly) before, and so they were very nervous when we [2] _____ (arrive) at Logan Airport to take our flight to Mexico. I [3] _____ (leave) them at the terminal building with instructions to get in line at the check-in desk while I [4] _____ (go) to park my car in the long-term parking lot. However, when I [5] _____ (get) to the check-in desk myself, they were nowhere in sight. I [6] _____ (look) for them everywhere until it suddenly occurred to me that they [7] _____ (already / check in) and they [8] _____ (wait) for me in the departure lounge. This was a real problem because I [9] _____ (give) my passport to my mother, so I couldn't check in.

I immediately [10] _____ (call) my parents on their cell phone. I was right; they [11] _____ (already / go) through to the departure lounge. They [12] _____ (wait) for me for almost half an hour at the gate. Luckily, my mom managed to find an understanding staff member who met me at the information desk with my passport!

5 PRONUNCIATION irregular past forms

a Put the irregular verbs in the box into the simple past. Then write them next to the simple past verbs 1–10 that have the same sound.

~~catch~~ cut fly meet pay say sing stand tell wake

1 bought	_caught_	6 spoke	_____
2 rang	_____	7 sold	_____
3 made	_____	8 knew	_____
4 let	_____	9 could	_____
5 shut	_____	10 read	_____

b **ONLINE** Listen and check. Then listen and repeat the simple past forms.

6 LISTENING

a **ONLINE** You are going to listen to an interview with a woman named Debbie who went on an exciting trip. Number the places on the map in the order she went to them.

_1_ Paris ___ Palau ___ Manila ___ Hong Kong

b Listen again and choose the right answers.

1 The Republic of Palau is…
   a to the east of the Philippines.
   b an island of the Philippines.
   c to the west of the Philippines.

2 The travel agent couldn't book all of Debbie's flights because…
   a the computer wasn't working.
   b she couldn't contact all the airlines.
   c one of the airlines was on strike.

3 When Debbie landed in Hong Kong, she…
   a went to a travel agent.
   b booked a flight to Manila.
   c bought the rest of her airline tickets.

4 The problem with the flight from Manila to Palau was…
   a the plane didn't carry any passengers.
   b there weren't any tickets left.
   c passengers weren't allowed to board at that airport.

5 Both Debbie and the pilot…
   a spoke the same language.
   b came from the same city.
   c had met before.

6 Debbie's friend met her at the airport in Palau because…
   a he had looked at the flight times.
   b she had called him.
   c he happened to be there.

c Listen again with the audio script on p.71 and try to guess the meaning of any words that you don't know. Then check in your dictionary.

USEFUL WORDS AND PHRASES

Learn these words and phrases.

air traffic controller /ɛr ˈtræfɪk kənˈtroʊlər/
life jacket /ˈlaɪf dʒækət/
safety demonstration /ˈseɪfti dɛmənˈstreɪʃn/
damage (noun and verb) /ˈdæmɪdʒ/
emergency /ɪˈmərdʒənsi/
engine /ˈɛndʒən/
flight announcement /flaɪt əˈnaʊnsmənt/
smuggle /ˈsmʌɡl/
wheelchair /ˈwiltʃɛr/
whistle /ˈwɪsl/

> Wanting to meet a writer because you like their books is like wanting to meet a duck because you like paté.
>
> *Margaret Atwood, Canadian author*

1 READING

a Read the article about different writers and their writing styles. Which one of them only works in the morning?

b Read the article again and match each writer (A–D) to a sentence.

Who says / said that…
1 he / she exercises after writing? _____
2 he / she has days when they do not write anything? _____
3 he / she writes a minimum number of pages every day? _____
4 he / she finds they can concentrate better when they are in bed? _____

c Look at the highlighted words and phrases in the text and try to figure out their meaning. Then use them to complete the sentences.
1 My sewing machine wasn't working, so I had to mend my skirt _____.
2 I gave my son the jug and told him to _____ with water.
3 I was so late I only had time to _____ my coat and rush out of the door.
4 The psychologist gave her some _____ advice on how to deal with her teenage son.
5 He finds it difficult to study at home because there are too many _____.
6 She's in a very confused _____, so she doesn't know whether to stay or go.

How do writers *write*?

All writers have their own particular ways of getting words down – a favorite pen, a special place, even a certain time of day. Four famous writers reveal their secrets.

Michael Morpurgo

British children's author

I had problems some years ago sitting at a desk because I got pains in my wrist and shoulder, so I decided to copy my writing hero Robert Louis Stevenson instead and found his way worked. Now, when I have a story in my head I go to bed with a small notebook, like the one children are given in elementary school, and fill it up. I keep my manuscripts in the refrigerator just in case the house burns down.

Suzanne Collins

American screenwriter and novelist

I grab some cereal and sit down to work as soon as possible. The more distractions I have to deal with before I actually begin writing, the harder focusing on the story becomes. Then I work until I'm tapped out*, usually sometime in the early afternoon. If I actually write three to five hours, that's a productive day. Some days all I do is stare at the wall. That can be productive, too, if you're working out character and plot problems. The rest of the time, I walk around with the story slipping in and out of my thoughts.

* tapped out – tired, exhausted

Haruki Murakami

Japanese author and translator

When I'm in the process of writing a novel, I get up at 4:00 a.m. and work for five to six hours. In the afternoon, I run for 6 miles or swim for 1 mile (or do both); then I read a bit and listen to some music. I go to bed at 9:00 p.m. I keep to this routine every day without variation. The repetition itself becomes the important thing; it's a form of hypnotism and it helps me reach a deeper state of mind.

Philip Pullman

British author

I sit down to write by hand, in ballpoint, on A4 narrow lined paper, after breakfast, and work through till lunch with a break for coffee and reading mail. Then I have lunch and watch *Neighbours** (invaluable). In the afternoon I read or take the dog for a walk or do something physically constructive. In the evening I finish the three pages, which is my daily task, or if I finished them in the morning, I do whatever journalism or reviewing or lecture-planning I have in hand.

* Neighbours – an Australian soap opera

2 GRAMMAR adverbs and adverbial phrases

a Right (✓) or wrong (✗)? Correct the wrong words.

1 Jack played extreme well, so he won the tennis final.
   extremely

2 Flying is a very safe way to travel. _____

3 My brother had an accident because he was driving too fast. _____

4 I speak Spanish really bad. Nobody can understand me when I speak it. _____

5 She works hardly and she's very ambitious, too. _____

6 Is this word spelled correctly here? _____

7 His parents have been happy married for almost forty years. _____

8 My friend sings good, but she'll never be a professional. _____

b Order the words to make sentences. Put the adverb in its usual position.

1 I / umbrella / an / had / luckily / taken
   Luckily I had taken an umbrella .

2 sick / hardly / daughter / is / my / ever
   _____ .

3 parents / next / are / his / retiring / year
   _____ .

4 boy / rude / teacher / was / to / the / extremely / his
   _____ .

5 eats / my / poorly / very / brother
   _____ .

6 is / James / apparently / divorced / getting
   _____ .

7 were / would / you / never / thought / I / have / thirty
   _____ .

c Put the adverbs / adverbial phrases in the correct place in each sentence.

   usually   immediately

1 He ⁄ gets up ⁄ when his alarm clock rings.
   (usually / immediately)

2 Although she studies, she goes to the library.
   (a lot / hardly ever)

3 I crashed my new car. (unfortunately / last week)

4 We should leave tomorrow. (ideally / early)

5 I can understand a word when people speak English. (hardly / quickly)

6 My brother forgot his girlfriend's birthday. (almost / yesterday)

7 It didn't rain while we were in Seattle. (surprisingly / at all)

8 We're tired because we went to bed late. (incredibly / last night)

3 VOCABULARY
adverbs and adverbial phrases

Circle the correct answer.

1 My father worked very hard / hardly all his life.

2 I haven't seen Tyler *late / lately*, have you?

3 I can't stand most TV shows, *specially / especially* reality shows.

4 Dave *near / nearly* broke his leg skiing in the Rockies.

5 Please don't tell me what happens because I haven't read the book *still / yet*.

6 I'm not going to Sam's party. I *hard / hardly* know him! He's your friend, not mine.

7 Do you *ever / even* wear jeans to work?

8 A Do your parents live *near / nearly* here?
   B No, they live about 30 miles away.

9 Ellie ate all her lunch, *ever / even* the vegetables!

10 Alan's feet are so big that his shoes are *especially / specially* made for him.

11 My cousin is a doctor and *right now / actually* she's working in Africa.

12 I can't wait to find out what happens *at the end / in the end* of this book.

4 PRONUNCIATION word stress

a Underline the stressed syllable and then write the adverb in the correct column.

ab	so	lute	ly	a	ppar	ent	ly	de	fi	nite	ly	e	ven	tu	a	lly
for	tu	nate	ly	i	mme	di	ate	ly	in	cre	di	bly	in	se	cure	ly
ob	vi	ous	ly	suc	cess	fu	lly	sur	pri	sing	ly	

stress on 1st syllable	stress on 2nd syllable	stress on 3rd syllable
absolutely		
_____	_____	_____
_____	_____	_____
_____	_____	_____
_____	_____	_____
_____	_____	_____

b **ONLINE** Listen and check. Then listen and repeat the adverbs.

5 LISTENING

a **ONLINE** Listen to five speakers talk about reading. Which two read the most? Speakers ___ and ___.

b Listen again and complete the table.

	What do they read?	Where do they read it?
Speaker 1	*best sellers*	_____
Speaker 2	_____	_____
Speaker 3	_____	_____
Speaker 4	_____	_____
Speaker 5	_____	_____

c Listen again with the audio script on p.71 and try to guess the meaning of any words that you don't know. Then check in your dictionary.

USEFUL WORDS AND PHRASES

Learn these words and phrases.

intention /ɪnˈtɛnʃn/
beg /bɛg/
recognize /ˈrɛkəgnaɪz/
bomb /bɑm/
couldn't believe my eyes /ˈkʊdnt bɪˈliv maɪ aɪz/
confrontation /kɑnfrənˈteɪʃn/
frantic /ˈfræntɪk/
slightly /ˈslaɪtli/

ONLINE FILE 3

Colloquial English Talking about... books

1 LOOKING AT LANGUAGE

Fill in the blanks to complete the mini dialogues.

1 **A** Which book have you enjoyed reading recently?
   B *The Hunger Games*. A<u>lright</u>, it was written for teenagers, but I really liked it.

2 **A** How do you like that e-reader I gave you?
   B I was worried I wouldn't use it, but a_____, it's very handy.

3 **A** Do you know anything about Ken Follett's books?
   B I think they're s_____ o_____ thrillers, aren't they?

4 **A** Have you ever read a Charles Dickens novel in English?
   B No way! I m_____, it would be too hard, wouldn't it?

5 **A** Did you enjoy *Crime and Punishment*?
   B Yes, although it was a little bit, y_____ kn_____, depressing in places.

6 **A** What do you think of the writer Dan Brown?
   B W_____, he's not a great writer, but I enjoy his books.

2 READING

a Read the article and (circle) the correct answers.

1 The article is about e-books in the *over* / (*under*) 18s e-book market.

2 *Fewer* / *More* seven- to twelve-year-olds have an e-reader than a computer.

3 The findings suggest that *fewer* / *more* children are likely to read e-books in the future.

4 Most children's books are bought *online* / *in stores*.

5 Older children are *more* / *less* attracted to e-books than their parents.

6 E-books are *more* / *less* popular with teenagers than other age groups.

7 Teenagers regard reading e-books as *an individual* / *a social* activity.

8 The research shows that children and teenagers still prefer *e-books* / *printed books*.

b Look at the highlighted words and phrases. What do you think they mean? Use your dictionary to look up their meaning and pronunciation.

Kids, teens, and e-books

Are young people embracing the new technology?

Publishers are closely monitoring the sales of printed books and e-books these days in order to adapt to an ever-changing market. Bearing in mind that today's children will be the consumers of the future, it is the under-18s that interest them most. Market research is carried out in this age group on a regular basis and new data suggests that this segment faces some very special challenges.

The first survey was conducted online among a thousand parents of children from the ages of zero to twelve. Disappointingly for digital booksellers, e-books still make up only 11 % of children's books. There are several reasons for this. First, a child needs to own a digital device to be able to read an e-book. The survey found that while 27 % of the kids of parents in the survey had their own computer and 25 % owned a smartphone, only 7 % currently possessed an e-reader. These figures are likely to increase in the future, however, as more children have access to a reading device. The parents in the survey said that they often share their digital devices with their kids and they are starting to hand them down when they upgrade to a newer model.

Another obstacle facing e-books in the children's market is the popularity of traditional bookstores. These are still the number one source of discovery for children's books and more than 85% of books are bought on impulse. Parents often prefer shopping in a bookstore because printed books are usually graded by age or level. They also make colorful presents for young children, while e-books lack the visual and tactile appeal. On the other hand, the research showed that the look and feel of a book becomes less important as children grow older. Seven- to twelve-year-olds say that e-books are "fun and cool" and they encourage them to read more, despite the fact that their parents would prefer them to read printed books.

The other segment that interests publishers is the young adult market. Teenagers today do most of their reading on smartphones and tablets, but this does not mean that they are in favor of e-books. A second online survey of a thousand 13- to 17-year-olds showed that teens are way behind all other age groups in e-book adoption. Sixty-six percent of young adults in the survey said that they prefer printed books to e-books, and only 8 % preferred e-books. The main reason for this resistance is that teenagers enjoy using technology as a social medium. Every day they read hundreds of short pieces about all kinds of different subjects and they share the most interesting with their friends. At this point, e-books cannot be shared or commented on and so they are not a social technology.

Surveys like these are of vital importance to publishers because they tell them about the latest trends in the market. In the case of the children's and young adult market, the two surveys have shown that printed books are still winning the race against e-books.

Only when the last tree has died, and the last river has been polluted, and the last fish has been caught, will we realize that we can't eat money.

Cree Indian saying

4A Eco-guilt

1 READING

a Read the article and choose the right answer.

How can Americans reduce their carbon footprints?

A By taking only two or three long airplane trips a year.

B By buying a lot of small products instead of a few big products.

C By reducing taxes on food, housing, and transportation.

D By spending less money on goods and services.

b Read the article again and choose a, b, or c.

1 The average American's carbon footprint is…
   a approximately eight times more than the global average carbon footprint per person.
   b approximately five times more than the global average carbon footprint per person.
   c approximately double the global average carbon footprint per person.

2 Americans with the lowest carbon footprints are usually …
   a people who have nowhere to live or eat.
   b people who serve as soldiers.
   c people who are unemployed.

3 A person who lives a simple lifestyle in the US has a high carbon footprint because…
   a he or she can't pay a tax to offset his or her carbon footprint.
   b the CO_2 footprint calculation is not divided equally among all US citizens.
   c he or she has access to public services paid for by the government.

4 The "rebound effect" …
   a has a negative impact on an individual's carbon footprint.
   b has a positive impact on an individual's carbon footprint.
   c has no impact on an individual's carbon footprint.

5 The writer's conclusion is that…
   a paying a carbon footprint tax is an easy solution.
   b finding a way to reduce the average US citizen's carbon footprint is more important than anything else to all Americans.
   c reducing the US carbon footprint is almost impossible.

Can We Make Our Carbon Footprints Smaller?

Our carbon footprint is the estimated amount of carbon dioxide (CO_2) given off as we go about our daily lives. While the global average carbon footprint is about 4 metric tons per person each year, Americans contribute approximately 20 metric tons of greenhouse gas per person each year. Compared to other countries, even those who use the least amount of energy in the US – for example, a person who lives off the grid – still contribute double the carbon emissions than the global average per person. And, not surprisingly, a person's carbon footprint increases in size as his or her income increases. So, the less you spend, the more environmentally friendly you are.

How is it possible that people in the US who live simple lifestyles, e.g., children or the homeless, make such large contributions to greenhouse gas emissions? The answer is simple: Each US citizen has access to various basic government services such as firefighting and police departments, road and bridge repair, libraries, jails and prisons, the military, etc. When these public services are divided equally among the entire US population, it significantly raises the carbon footprint per person. In fact, according to a study conducted by the Massachusetts Institute of Technology, the lowest carbon footprint that can be calculated for a person living in the US is 8.5 metric tons. And shockingly, this carbon footprint corresponds to a homeless person who sleeps in public shelters and eats in soup kitchens.

While it is admirable to make changes in lifestyle to reduce a carbon footprint, in reality, it is very difficult to do. The MIT study revealed that a "rebound effect" occurred when someone made an effort to reduce his or her carbon footprint. Take the example of a person who made the deliberate choice to buy a hybrid car instead of a large SUV to save money on gas costs. Very often that person would use the money he or she saved to do something else, e.g., take a long airplane trip. In this case, just one long airplane trip produces more CO_2 emissions than driving the large SUV for a year. This ends up having a negative impact on a person's carbon footprint by making it bigger!

Can Americans reduce their carbon footprints? According to the study, it IS possible, but it would require lifestyle changes such as giving up long-distance travel and buying fewer smartphones, tablets, and MP3 players that have large

energy costs to produce and deliver. The most drastic way to lower the average American's US carbon footprint is to add a CO_2 tax on food, housing, and transportation, and most Americans don't want their taxes raised. Unless we can find a way to reduce our carbon footprints, the price we may ultimately have to pay is much higher than the amount Americans will ever have to pay in taxes.

c Look at the highlighted words and phrases in the text and try to figure out their meaning. Then match to definitions 1–8.

1 not using the public supplies of electricity, gas, or water _____

2 the powerful effect that something has on someone or something _____

3 money that you have to pay the government so that it can pay for public services _____

4 sent into the air _____

5 not harming the world around us _____

6 extreme in a way that has serious effect on something _____

7 done on purpose _____

8 when a situation is different from what has just been said or from what people believe _____

2 VOCABULARY the weather

a Circle the one that doesn't belong.

1 below zero   chilly   freezing   (pouring)
2 settled   pouring   drizzling   showers
3 boiling   damp   mild   warm
4 fog   mist   smog   thunder
5 blizzard   hailstorm   breeze   monsoon

b Complete the sentences with a suitable word.

1 We're having a h*eat wave*. It's not usually so hot at this time of year.

2 The weather is very ch_____ right now. One minute it's raining and the next the sun comes out.

3 People say that there may be a fl_____ if the river continues rising.

4 In some areas it was raining and in others there was h_____. The balls of ice were enormous!

5 There will be h_____ rain this morning, so drive carefully.

6 The government wants us to save water because of the dr_____.

7 In India, m_____ season usually lasts until October.

8 The l_____ lit up the sky during the thunderstorm.

9 I just took a shower 30 minutes ago and I'm sweating already – it's so h_____!

c Match each adjective to a noun.

1 strong   a skies
2 cool   b fog
3 clear   c rain
4 sunny   d periods
5 heavy   e breeze
6 thick   f sunshine
7 icy   g roads
8 bright   h winds

3 GRAMMAR
future perfect and future continuous

a Circle the correct form.

1 If this hot weather continues, forecasters say we *will have* | *will have had* | *will be having* a drought.

2 We *will have* | *will have had* | *will be having* six meetings by the end of today.

3 I've decided that in the future I *will take* | *will have taken* | *will be taking* the train to work.

4 Please don't call between one and two o'clock because we *will have* | *will have had* | *will be having* lunch.

5 Anna *will study* | *will have studied* | *will be studying* at college the next time we see her.

6 We *will buy* | *will have bought* | *will be buying* a beach house if we can sell the condo.

b Complete the sentences with the future perfect or future continuous form of the verb in parentheses.

1 By the end of this month, we*'ll have moved* (move) to our new house, so you can come and stay after that.

2 This time tomorrow my parents _____ (fly) over the Atlantic on their way to London.

3 Rob's exams are in May, so he _____ (take) them all by June first.

4 Hopefully you _____ (read) the book I lent you by the next time we see each other.

5 If the game starts at 7:00 p.m., we _____ (play) until 8:45 at least.

6 By this time next year, they _____ (build) the new road and we'll be able to get to work much quicker.

7 When do you think you _____ (finish) paying your mortgage?

8 Don't call me tomorrow morning because I _____ (drive) to Los Angeles.

9 It's been raining all day, but hopefully it _____ (stop) by tomorrow. We were planning to have a picnic.

10 _____ (you go) to the supermarket later?

4 PRONUNCIATION vowel sounds

a Which words have the same vowel sound? Complete the chart with the words from the box.

~~drizzling~~	drought	heat wave
lightning	pouring	thunder

fish	tree	owl
chilly	breeze	showers
drizzling	_____	_____

horse	up	bike
warm	flood	bright
_____	_____	_____

b **ONLINE** Listen and check. Then listen and repeat.

5 LISTENING

a **ONLINE** Listen to a news report about paraglider Ewa Wisnierska. What kind of difficult weather did she experience? _____

b Listen again and answer the questions.

1 In which country did the incident take place?
2 Why couldn't Ewa Wisnierska avoid the problem?
3 What temperature did Ewa experience during her ascent?
4 What did she see during her ascent?
5 What could she hear?
6 How long was she unconscious?
7 Where did she land?
8 How long did she spend in the hospital?
9 Where was the other paraglider from?
10 Did he survive?

c Listen again with the audio script on p.71 and try to guess the meaning of any words that you don't know. Then check in your dictionary.

USEFUL WORDS AND PHRASES

Learn these words and phrases.

banned /bænd/
cut down (trees) /kʌt daʊn/
extreme weather /ɪkˈstrim ˈwɛðər/
heat wave /ˈhit weɪv/
install /ɪnˈstɔl/
reusable /riˈyuzəbl/
recyclable /riˈsaɪkləbl/
run out (of gas) /rʌn aʊt/
solar panels /ˈsoʊlər ˈpænlz/
weather forecast /ˈwɛðər ˈfɔrkæst/

4B Are you a risk taker?

1 READING

a Read the article and number the paragraphs in the correct order.

b Read the article again. Mark the sentences **T** (true) or **F** (false).

1 Most people think that boys take more risks than girls.   *T*

2 In the past, men had to pay more than women to insure their cars.   —

3 A third of the girls in the survey said that they replied to text messages while driving.   —

4 In general, girls use cell phones when they are driving more than boys.   —

5 The second survey involved both men and women.   —

6 New mothers are the safest drivers of all.   —

7 Women now have to pay higher insurance rates than men in some countries.   —

c Look at the highlighted words and phrases in the text and try to figure out their meaning. Then use them to complete the sentences.

1 Some people have different personalities when they're _____ of a car.

2 I didn't _____ to your text message because my phone battery died.

3 The police arrested everyone who had been _____ in the fight.

4 The banks are raising interest _____ from 1.5 % to 2 %.

5 The cuts are _____ education. There will also be less money for health care.

6 An example of his _____ is when he drove on the freeway doing 110 miles per hour.

7 My parents _____ me in my choice of career.

8 Zane wears shorts all the time _____ how bad the weather is.

DANGEROUS DRIVERS

☐ **A** What is more, cell phone use while driving is not confined to young women. A child protection group in the US recently did a survey of the habits of new mothers in the car. The results of this survey are similarly shocking. Of the 2,396 mothers who took part, 78 % admitted talking on the phone when they were driving with their babies in the car. Twenty-six percent said that they regularly texted or checked their emails. Not surprisingly, nearly 10 % of the mothers interviewed had been involved in a car crash. These results show that new mothers behave almost as badly on the road as teenagers.

☐*1* **B** It is widely accepted that boys are bigger risk takers than girls. More men than women take part in risky sports and men are more likely to be responsible for reckless driving. Until now, this factor has been reflected in car insurance policies, which have always required men to pay higher rates than women. However, recent research has shown that this belief may no longer be correct.

☐ **C** With statistics like these, it is hardly surprising that insurance companies are reconsidering the policies they offer. And they are being backed by some countries around the world. The European Court of Justice, for example, has recently passed a measure that prohibits insurance companies from taking gender into account when calculating the cost of an insurance policy. The change serves to make one thing very clear: a distracted driver is a dangerous driver, no matter what sex they are.

☐ **D** A survey of 2,000 young drivers about the risks they take on the road revealed some surprising figures. More than a third of the girls who took part admitted that they regularly read text messages from friends and family members while driving. More than a quarter of these girls admitted answering the texts while they were behind the wheel. In contrast, the boys did not seem so concerned about who was trying to contact them. A much smaller number admitted to reading texts on the road, and only 10 percent said that they would try to respond to the message before stopping the car.

2 VOCABULARY expressions with *take*

Complete the sentences with a suitable word.

1 My mother takes good c_are___ of herself and still looks great for her age.

2 Katie believes in women's rights. She takes gender equality very s_____.

3 My son loves drama, so he always takes p_____ in the school play.

4 My husband takes a_____ his father – they're both passionate about basketball.

5 My girlfriend is very sensible. She doesn't like taking r_____.

6 You don't have to finish this today. There's no hurry. You can take your t_____.

7 I'm taking u_____ yoga because I need to learn to relax.

8 Let's take ad_____ of the nice weather and have a barbecue.

9 We didn't take the rush hour traffic into acc_____, so we almost missed our flight.

10 The Coachella Valley Music and Arts Festival usually takes p_____ over two weekends in the middle of April.

3 GRAMMAR zero and first conditionals and future time clauses

a Complete the sentences with the present or the future (*will* / *won't*) form of the verbs in the box.

not answer	be	cook	~~eat~~
not get	go	not move	not rain

1 If you _eat___ too many calories, you gain weight.

2 Plants die if they _____ enough water.

3 I _____ and see the doctor if I don't feel better tomorrow.

4 If it _____ soon, there will be a drought.

5 Some dogs bite if they _____ scared.

6 If we don't sell our house, we _____ .

7 If Justin _____ tonight, Karen will be very happy.

8 My sister _____ the phone if she's watching a movie on TV.

b Complete the sentences with the correct form of the verbs.

1 *Bring__* your swimsuit if you want to use the pool. (bring)

2 Don't call them now. They _____ lunch. (have)

3 I _____ if those people don't stop talking. (complain)

4 If you tell me what's wrong, I _____ anything. (not say)

5 If everything goes according to plan, we _____ work early today. (finish)

6 I won't be able to talk to you if I _____ when you call. (drive)

7 If you _____ Dan Brown's new book yet, I'll buy you a copy for your birthday. (not read)

8 You'll get wet if you _____ an umbrella with you. (not take)

c Fill in the blanks in each sentence so that it means the same as the sentence (or sentences) before. Use a time expression from the box and no more than two other words.

after	as soon as	before
in case	unless	until	~~when~~

1 I'll go to New York and I'll stay with some friends. I'll stay with some friends _when I go_ to New York.

2 My boyfriend will arrive at his hotel. He'll call me immediately.
My boyfriend will call me _____ at his hotel.

3 We'll arrive in time for lunch if the traffic isn't bad.
We'll arrive in time for lunch _____ is bad.

4 I'm going to call my husband. He might forget his doctor's appointment.
I'm going to call my husband _____ his doctor's appointment.

5 She's going to pack her suitcase. Then she'll go to bed.
She's going to pack her suitcase _____ to bed.

6 They'll get married and then they'll live together.
They won't live together _____ married.

7 I'll do my Pilates and then I'll take a shower.
I'll take a shower _____ my Pilates.

4 PRONUNCIATION word stress

a Underline the stress in the words.

1 ac|ci|dent	3 ad|van|tage	5 con|trol	7 in|sur|ance	9 ris|ky
2 a|ccount	4 a|tti|tude	6 de|ci|sion	8 night|mare	10 safe|ty

b [ONLINE] Listen and check. Then listen and repeat the words. <u>C</u>opy the <u>rhy</u>thm.

5 LISTENING

a [ONLINE] Listen to part of a radio program where Andy Evans talks about bungee jumping and complete the sentences. You sometimes have to write more than one word.

1 The first bungee jumps originated on the island of Vanuatu, which is in the _____.

2 Young men called "land divers" used to jump off platforms with vines tied to _____.

3 In 1979 Chris Baker and three friends jumped off the Clifton Suspension Bridge in the city of _____, using a rope called a "bungee."

4 Immediately after the team had jumped, they _____ by police.

5 However, people carried on doing bungee jumps, especially in _____.

6 Many people did jumps from the _____ _____ in San Francisco.

7 Some of the jumps were sponsored by _____.

8 Fatalities sometimes occur when people use a bungee that is _____.

9 Calculations and fittings should be _____ -checked before each jump.

b Listen again with the audio script on p.72 and try to guess the meaning of any words that you don't know. Then check in your dictionary.

USEFUL WORDS AND PHRASES

Learn these words and phrases.

addicted to /əˈdɪktəd tə/	fatal (accident) /ˈfeɪtl/	in advance /ɪn ədˈvæns/
a sense of /ə sens əv/	for charity /fər ˈtʃærəti/	potentially /pəˈtenʃli/
at the last minute /æt ðə læst ˈmɪnət/	get caught (by the police) /ɡet kɔt/	risky /ˈrɪski/
break the speed limit /breɪk ðə spid ˈlɪmət/	get straight to the point /ɡet streɪt tə ðə pɔɪnt/	take a risk /teɪk ə rɪsk/

1 READING

a Read the story quickly. How did Nicholas Joy survive the freezing conditions of Sugarloaf Mountain?

b Read the story again and choose the right answer.

1 Sugarloaf Mountain is popular with skiers because…
   a it is easy to get to.
   b it is free on the weekend.
   c it is in a beautiful area.

2 Nicholas and his father separated because Nicholas wanted to…
   a go a different way.
   b sit down and take a rest.
   c meet some friends at the parking lot.

3 Nicholas knew how to make a snow cave because…
   a his father had taught him.
   b he had seen someone do it on TV.
   c he had taken a survival course.

4 The first thing Joseph Paul did when he found Nicholas was to…
   a call his parents.
   b give him some food.
   c take him back to the resort.

5 Skiers who get lost at Sugarloaf…
   a have usually left the official trail.
   b usually make their own snow caves.
   c usually have good survival skills.

c Find the words and phrases in the text to match definitions 1–8.

1 people who are very interested in an activity (*paragraph 1*) _____

2 a more direct way to get somewhere (*paragraph 2*) _____

3 made someone aware of something (*paragraph 2*) _____

4 a small river (*paragraph 3*) _____

5 a path through the woods or fields (*paragraph 4*) _____

6 in a position where the arms, legs, and head are close to the body (*paragraph 4*) _____

7 a phrase meaning you aren't allowed to go there (*paragraph 5*) _____

8 survive (*paragraph 5*) _____

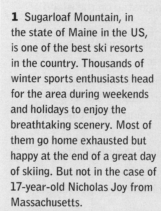

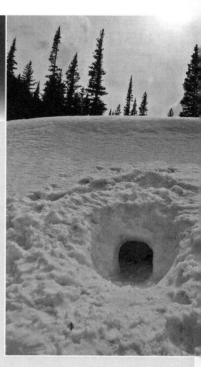

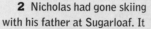

Night on a bare mountain

1 Sugarloaf Mountain, in the state of Maine in the US, is one of the best ski resorts in the country. Thousands of winter sports enthusiasts head for the area during weekends and holidays to enjoy the breathtaking scenery. Most of them go home exhausted but happy at the end of a great day of skiing. But not in the case of 17-year-old Nicholas Joy from Massachusetts.

2 Nicholas had gone skiing with his father at Sugarloaf. It was a Sunday, and they were on their way back down the mountain when Nicholas saw a shortcut. He decided to take the shortcut while his father continued down the official path. They arranged to meet back at the parking lot for the drive home. And that was the last his father saw him that day because Nicholas didn't turn up at the parking lot. After waiting for what he considered to be a reasonable time, Nicholas's worried father alerted the authorities. A massive search party was launched, but it soon began to snow heavily. Eventually, the search was called off.

3 Meanwhile, Nicholas was desperate. He had gotten hopelessly lost, and he realized that he was going to have to spend the night on the mountain. Fortunately, he is a big fan of survival shows so he knew how to make a snow cave. He found a safe place to build his cave and made a huge pile of snow with his skis. Then, he made a tunnel into the snow and dug out a hole to sit in. He covered the bottom with fallen pine branches and lay down inside. Whenever he was thirsty, he left the cave and drank water from a nearby stream. Then he returned to his cave and waited to be found.

4 Rescue came two days later in the form of snowmobiler Joseph Paul. Mr. Paul was riding along a trail about 4 miles from the resort when he spotted Nicholas's snow cave. He got off his snowmobile, inspected the cave, and found Nicholas curled up inside. After giving the hungry teenager some cheese crackers and peanuts, he took Nicholas back to the resort to be reunited with his relieved parents.

5 An official at Sugarloaf confirmed that two or three groups of skiers get lost on the mountain each year. Like Nicholas, they are usually found in areas that are out of bounds. However, few of the rescued skiers are in such good shape because they lack his knowledge of survival skills. Tragically, some of them do not make it through the night.

2 VOCABULARY feelings

a How would you feel in these situations? Complete the crossword.

Clues across ➡

1 Your daughter won a dance competition.
4 It's pouring rain and a friend offers to drive you to your home.
6 You have an exam tomorrow.
7 You just told your parents that you failed an exam.

Clues down ⬇

2 You weren't offered the job after you went for an interview.
3 Someone told you that your new hairstyle makes you look old.
4 You forgot your best friend's birthday yesterday.
5 You're studying abroad and you're missing your family.

¹p	r	o	²u	d

(crossword grid with answers)

b Replace the underlined words with a suitable adjective from the box.

astonished	bewildered	delighted
devastated	horrified	stunned	~~thrilled~~

1 We are <u>very excited</u> to be going on a cruise around the world. _thrilled_
2 My mom was <u>very confused</u> by the touch screen on her new phone. _____
3 People were <u>extremely shocked and disgusted</u> when they heard about the terrorist attack. _____
4 Andy was <u>amazed</u> when his parents gave him a car for his birthday. _____
5 She was <u>so surprised she couldn't react</u> when she saw the fire damage. _____
6 Olivia was <u>incredibly happy</u> when she got promoted. _____
7 My brother was <u>extremely upset</u> when his wife left him. _____

c Complete the sentences with the words in the box.

couldn't believe his eyes	down	jumping for joy
~~scared stiff~~	sick and tired of	worn out

1 Harriet was _scared stiff_ when she saw a mugger coming toward her.
2 I'm _____ always having to tell my husband to clean up.

3 My sister was a little _____ after her interview went badly.
4 He was absolutely _____ after running almost 15 miles.

5 He _____ when his favorite celebrity re-tweeted him on Twitter.
6 I was _____ when I got accepted to my top choice college.

3 GRAMMAR unreal conditionals

a Circle the correct form.

1 Our boss *was* | *(would be)* more popular if he didn't take himself so seriously.
2 I would have gotten cold if I *didn't take* | *hadn't taken* a jacket.
3 You *hadn't have* | *wouldn't have* sprained your ankle if you'd been looking where you were going.
4 I'd really miss you if you *went* | *would go* away.
5 Matt *had* | *would have* more friends if he didn't complain all the time.
6 I *had been* | *would have been* really disappointed if I hadn't gotten the job.
7 You *didn't get* | *wouldn't get* blisters if you were wearing shoes that actually fit you well.
8 We wouldn't have come to Bangkok if we *knew* | *had known* it was the monsoon season.
9 Emma wouldn't be so stressed out if she *didn't have* | *wouldn't have* so much work.
10 We wouldn't have gotten lost if we *had stayed* | *would have stayed* on the hiking trail.

b Write second and third conditional sentences.

1 We don't go hiking because we don't have much free time.
If we ___had___ more free time, ___we'd go hiking___ more often.

2 There wasn't much snow, so we didn't make a snowman.
We _____ a snowman if there _____ more snow.

3 I didn't know the water was so cold, so I jumped in.
I _____ into the water if I _____ it was so cold.

4 He doesn't pass his driver's test because he gets so nervous.
If he _____ so nervous, he _____ his driver's test.

5 We got lost because we didn't follow the trail.
If we _____ the trail, we _____ .

6 You get sunburned because you don't use enough sunscreen.
If you _____ more sunscreen, you _____ sunburned.

7 They hadn't read the book, so they didn't understand the movie.
They _____ the movie if they _____ the book.

8 I don't earn a lot of money, so I can't buy my own house.
I _____ my own house if I _____ more money.

4 PRONUNCIATION word stress

a Complete the table with the words according to the stressed syllable. Then underline the words where "ed" adds another syllable to the word.

| a\|sto\|nished | be\|wil\|dered | de\|ligh\|ted | de\|va\|sta\|ted |
| dis\|a\|ppoin\|ted | horr\|i\|fied | o\|ffen\|ded | o\|ver\|whelmed |

stress on 1st syllable	stress on 2nd syllable	stress on 3rd syllable
_____	_astonished_	_____
_____	_____	_____
_____	_____	_____
_____	_____	_____

b ONLINE Listen and check. Then listen and repeat. Copy the rhythm.

c ONLINE Listen and circle the word where -ed is pronounced differently.

1 thrilled   confused   (excited)   (-ed = /ɪd/ not /d/)
2 depressed   exhausted   offended
3 shocked   astonished   surprised
4 relieved   frustrated   terrified
5 disgusted   irritated   stunned

d Listen and repeat the words.

5 LISTENING

a ONLINE Listen to a firefighter giving a talk on house fires at a community center and complete the notes.

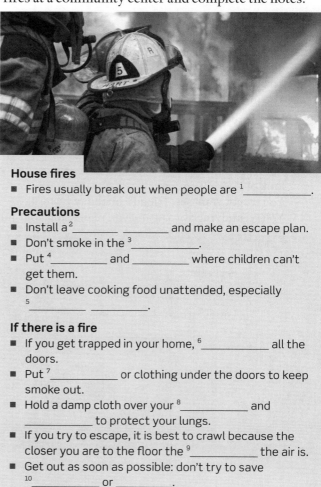

House fires
- Fires usually break out when people are [1] _____ .

Precautions
- Install a [2] _____ _____ and make an escape plan.
- Don't smoke in the [3] _____ .
- Put [4] _____ and _____ where children can't get them.
- Don't leave cooking food unattended, especially [5] _____ _____ .

If there is a fire
- If you get trapped in your home, [6] _____ all the doors.
- Put [7] _____ or clothing under the doors to keep smoke out.
- Hold a damp cloth over your [8] _____ and _____ to protect your lungs.
- If you try to escape, it is best to crawl because the closer you are to the floor the [9] _____ the air is.
- Get out as soon as possible: don't try to save [10] _____ or _____ .

b Listen again with the audio script on p.72 and try to guess the meaning of any words that you don't know. Then check in your dictionary.

USEFUL WORDS AND PHRASES

Learn these words and phrases.

challenge /ˈtʃæləndʒ/
keep calm /kip kɑm/
life or death situation /laɪf ɔr dɛθ sɪtʃuˈeɪʃn/
overcome /oʊvərˈkʌm/
panic /ˈpænɪk/
remote /rɪˈmoʊt/
rescue /ˈrɛskyu/
set off (on a journey) /sɛt ɔf/
survival /sərˈvaɪvl/
task /tæsk/

5B It drives me crazy!

1 GRAMMAR *wish + would*

a Use the words to write sentences with *wish + would*.

1 I / that man / stop coughing
   I wish that man would stop coughing.

2 I / you / wash the dishes

   _____

3 I / my sister / not borrow / my clothes

   _____

4 I / our neighbors / not park / outside our house

   _____

5 I / my grandma / get a hearing aid

   _____

6 I / the bus / come

   _____

b Write sentences with *wish + would*.

1 My boss really annoys me. She shouts all the time.
   I wish _my boss wouldn't shout all the time_____.

2 I'm fed up with my brother using my computer.
   I wish _____.

3 I'm really angry. You never help with the housework.
   I wish _____ sometimes.

4 I can't stand it when my son stays in bed all day.
   I wish _____.

5 My ex-boyfriend is driving me crazy! He calls me every day.
   I wish _____.

6 I hate it when you leave the bathroom messy.
   I wish _____.

2 VOCABULARY

-ed / -ing adjectives and related verbs

Complete the sentences with an adjective or a verb made from the word in **bold**.

1 These dark, winter days are very _depressing_.
  depress

2 Taking care of my sister's three small children is
  _____ for my parents. **exhaust**

3 She's a little bit _____ right now because
  she has too much work. **stress**

4 It really _____ me when people talk loudly
  on their cell phones. **infuriate**

5 Ethan was so _____ when he failed his
  driver's test. **disappoint**

6 I can't find my passport, which is a little
  _____. **worry**

7 My girlfriend is scared of flying. The idea of
  getting on a plane _____ her. **terrify**

8 We were _____ when we received a
  surprise visit from some old friends. **delight**

9 My son is a terrible loser. Not winning something
  really _____ him. **frustrate**

10 I was so _____ when I called your
   boyfriend by the wrong name. **embarrass**

11 It _____ me when my husband asks me
   where his clothes are. **annoy**

12 His first visit to the theater _____ him to
   take up acting. **inspire**

33

3 READING

a Read the article. Complete it with the missing sentences.

A When journalist Kathryn Schulz was 29, she decided to get a tattoo

B Since then, Ms. Schulz has found two ways of dealing with her regret

C Apart from these four components, Ms. Schulz also felt pain

D Despite not having the effect that she had intended, Ms. Schulz's tattoo has served to remind her of something else

E Ms. Schulz experienced all four components of regret that night

F Ms. Schulz's tattoo is a compass

b Read the whole text again and mark the sentences **T** (true) or **F** (false).

1 Kathryn Schulz had had no regrets until she got a tattoo.   _T_

2 The first emotion Ms. Schulz felt that night was a kind of confusion.   ____

3 By the time she got home, her wrist had stopped hurting.   ____

4 Ms. Schulz isn't the only American who regrets having a tattoo.   ____

5 In Ms. Schulz's opinion, regret usually disappears over time.   ____

6 When Ms. Schulz shows people her tattoo, they are usually horrified.   ____

7 Ms. Schultz wanted a tattoo that reminded her of the places she traveled to.   ____

8 She thinks regrets teach us to accept our mistakes. ____

c Look at the highlighted words and phrases in the text and try to figure out their meaning. Then match them to definitions 1–10.

1 happening many times _____

2 a refusal to accept that something unpleasant has happened _____

3 with a mistake which means that it is not perfect _____

4 happening at exactly the same time as something else _____

5 purposes or aims _____

6 thinking too much about one particular thing _____

7 the importance of something _____

8 accept something unpleasant or difficult _____

9 confusion and surprise _____

10 a basic general idea _____

Don't regret regrets

[1] _A_ . Unfortunately, she regretted getting it as soon as she left the tattoo shop. Until then, she had been proud of leading a life without regrets. She had gone through life working on the principle that you should always look forward and never look back. But that night, she remembers feeling regret for the very first time.

[2] ____ . The first one was denial and she spent the first few hours saying to herself, "Make it go away!" The second was a feeling of bewilderment in which she kept on asking herself, "How could I have done that?" The third was a desire to punish herself, something along the lines of "I could kick myself." The fourth is something that psychologists call perseveration. This is the habit of focussing obsessively and repeatedly on the exact same thing. A person who is feeling regret has the first three components going around in their head again and again.

[3] ____ ; not only the physical pain of her tattooed wrist, but the emotional pain of knowing that she had done something incredibly stupid.

[4] ____ . The first is to take comfort in the fact that she is not alone. Figures show that around 17 % of Americans regret getting tattoos at some point in their lives. The second is to learn to laugh at herself. Humor and black humor play a fundamental role in helping us come to terms with our regret. Apart from that, Ms. Schulz recognizes the value of sitting back and waiting for the pain of regret to go away. *Time heals all wounds* as the saying goes, and in the case of regret, this is most certainly true.

[5] ____ . Most people who see it are disappointed, because they don't think it is that bad; the problem is that she doesn't like it. She got the tattoo when she was traveling and she was worried that she would forget some of the lessons that she had learned during that time. It is a lesson that she wants to share with other people. For her, the compass represented the two ideas in one image.

[6] ____ . It reminds her how important it is to keep on exploring, and simultaneously how important it is to know where you're heading in life. Ms. Schulz believes that if we have goals and dreams and if we love people, we should feel pain when things go wrong. In her view, we need to learn to love the flawed things that we create and to be able to forgive ourselves for creating them. Ms. Schulz says that her experience has taught her that regret doesn't exist to remind us that we did badly; instead it is there to remind us that we know that we can do better.

4 GRAMMAR
wish + simple past or past perfect

Complete the sentences with the simple past or past perfect form of a verb from the box.

not be	can	not eat	get up	~~have~~
live	offer	not spent	not work	wear

1 Public transportation is terrible around here. I wish I ___*had*___ a car.
2 I miss my parents. I wish they _____ nearby.
3 I'm going to be late. I wish I _____ earlier.
4 I hardly ever see my boyfriend. I wish he _____ on the weekends.
5 I'm really disappointed. I wish they _____ me the job.
6 I'd love to live in Paris. I wish I _____ speak French.
7 I'm broke. I wish I _____ all my money.
8 The weekend has flown by. I wish it _____ Monday tomorrow.
9 I feel sick. I wish I _____ that seafood last night.
10 I'm cold. I wish I _____ a sweater.

5 PRONUNCIATION *-ed* adjective endings

a **ONLINE** Listen and write the adjectives in the correct column according to the pronunciation of *-ed*.

~~amazed~~	astonished	confused	disappointed
embarrassed	frustrated	infuriated	inspired
offended	shocked	stressed	terrified

d **d**og	**t** **t**ie	/ɪd/
amazed	_____	_____
_____	_____	_____
_____	_____	_____
_____	_____	_____

b Listen and repeat the adjectives paying attention to the pronunciation of the *-ed* endings.

6 LISTENING

a **ONLINE** Listen to a couple, Daniel and Ana, discussing the characteristics of different members of their families. Write **M** (Daniel's mom) or **D** (Daniel's dad). There are two adjectives that you don't need to use.

Who is…?
- ☐ unwell
- ☐ helpful
- ☐ stubborn
- ☐ selfish
- ☐ critical
- ☐ insincere

b Listen again. What examples does Ana give of Daniel's parents' behavior?

_____

_____

c Listen again with the audio script on p.72 and try to guess the meaning of any words that you don't know. Then check in your dictionary.

USEFUL WORDS AND PHRASES

Learn these words and phrases.

argue with /ˈɑrgyu wɪθ/
career /kəˈrɪr/
give up (an activity, e.g., watching TV) /gɪv ʌp/
learn from (a mistake) /lərn frʌm/
make up (after an argument) /meɪk ʌp/
It drives me crazy /ɪt draɪvz mi ˈkreɪzi/
love life /lʌv laɪf/
on average /ɑn ˈævrɪdʒ/
regret (doing something) /rɪˈgrɛt/
regrets (n) /rɪˈgrɛts/

ONLINE FILE 5

1 LOOKING AT LANGUAGE

Circle the right adverbs in the mini dialogues.

1 **A** How do you recycle your organic waste?
   B We don't. *Ideally / Obviously / Unfortunately,* it's impossible to do that where we live.

2 **A** Who's in charge of emptying the waste baskets in your house?
   B *Amazingly / Gradually / Sadly,* my teenage son always takes the trash out.

3 **A** How do you dispose of old electrical devices?
   B *Actually / Eventually / Unfortunately,* it's not usually a problem because I rarely buy new ones.

4 **A** What kind of things do you recycle?
   B *Amazingly / Apparently / Basically,* we try to recycle as much as we can.

5 **A** Can you see any problems with recycling?
   B *Actually / Anyway / Obviously,* you need four different bins in the kitchen, but apart from that, it's easy.

6 **A** What happened to that beautiful old vase you had?
   B *Generally / Sadly / Strangely* it broke, so we had to throw it away.

7 **A** Have they come to empty the recycling bins yet?
   B No, they haven't. They always come on Mondays, but *basically / in fact / strangely* they haven't been here yet today.

2 READING

a Read the article about the zero waste policy in San Francisco. Complete it with the missing sentences. There is one sentence you do not need to use.

A Then there is the question of penalties.

B When recycling was first introduced, it was discovered that the largest remaining kind of trash was leftover food.

C All kinds of trash can be found in these places, from broken toys to unwanted CDs, and a lot of items that could have been recycled.

D One of the few things that people are warned against putting here are plastic bags, which are not biodegradable at all.

E He wants the city to achieve 100 % zero waste.

F The most commonly recycled items are glass bottles.

b Look at the highlighted words and phrases. What do you think they mean? Use your dictionary to look up their meaning and pronunciation.

San Francisco: Zero-Waste City

Each year, Americans throw away about 250 million tons of garbage. That's roughly 4 pounds per person per day, most of which ends up in a landfill site. [1]____ As well as being an eyesore, landfills create environmental damage and emit harmful greenhouse gases, which have been shown to contribute to climate change. These concerns have prompted San Francisco and a handful of other cities to aim for a once-unthinkable goal: zero waste.

In 2009, San Francisco became the first city in the country to require that residents and businesses alike separate from their trash biodegradable items, like food scraps, and recyclable goods, like paper, metals, and plastic, into separate bins. And that has led to a big reduction in the amount of garbage headed to the landfill. The city's new laws have helped to keep 80 % of its waste away from landfills, when the national average is 35 %. However, the city mayor, Ed Lee, wants to go even further. [2]____

San Francisco's 80-year-old private garbage company has recently invented a new name for itself: Recology. [3]____ This can be used to make a substance called compost, which can be added to soil to help plants grow. So, Recology set about building a new composting facility on an enormous complex northeast of San Francisco. Here they turn all of the city's organic waste into rich compost that is used by some of the nation's best vineyards. In the rest of the country, where composting is a rarity, 97 % of food waste is disposed of in landfills.

Surprisingly, it isn't only food that residents are told to put into their compost bins; they are encouraged to put in all kinds of other garbage as well. This includes packaging where meat has been sold, food wrappings, paper napkins, tissues, used paper plates, and even milk cartons. In the right conditions, paper will biodegrade in two to four weeks. Compost bins provide these conditions because they are warm and moist. [4]____ However, Ed Lee has found a solution to this problem, too: he has banned them from the city.

Not all San Franciscans are enthusiastic about Ed Lee's recycling policy because they say it is costing them more. Since last year, residents have had to pay for their recycling and compost bins, as well as their trash bins. [5]____ Those who refuse to sort their garbage can face fines ranging from $100 to $1,000. Teams of workers from the city go around knocking on doors of residents who, without realizing it, have had their garbage cans inspected by auditors early in the morning. The idea is to educate people on composting and recycling and answer any questions they may have. So far, no fines have been imposed and only warnings have been given out. And city officials say that the more people know about zero waste, the more eager they are to support the policy.

Music expresses that which cannot be put into words and that which cannot remain silent.

Victor Hugo, poet, novelist, and dramatist

6A Music and emotion

1 READING

a Read the article quickly and answer the questions.

1 What danger does the article refer to?

2 Who is affected by the problem?

b Read the article again and mark the sentences **T** (true) or **F** (false).

1 The writer's mother didn't want her to go to the concert. ___*T*___

2 The music at the concert was louder than the sound of a jet plane taking off. ___

3 After the concert, the writer had no symptoms of hearing damage. ___

4 The writer had problems with her hearing at work, but not at home. ___

5 The writer pretended that she could hear what a person at the party was saying. ___

6 Despite her problems, the writer can still hear sounds at the bottom range of the scale. ___

7 The doctors told her that her hearing would eventually recover. ___

8 Now the writer wears a device in one ear to help her hear better. ___

9 According to the writer, most people don't take the dangers of hearing loss seriously. ___

c Look at the highlighted words and phrases in the text and try to figure out their meaning. Then match to definitions 1–8.

1 obviously _____

2 showed annoyance at something that was said _____

3 not fashionable _____

4 affect your senses in a way that is very unpleasant or uncomfortable _____

5 very annoying _____

6 in the end we discover _____

7 sounds that you can hear, but you are not listening to _____

8 become worse _____

The hidden dangers of rock music

Twenty-two years ago as I left the house to go to see Motörhead – known at the time as "the loudest band in the world" – my mother's words followed me out of the door: "You'll ruin your hearing one day!" At the time, I rolled my eyes dramatically, and proceeded to assault my ears with 140 decibels of noise, which I now know is ten decibels above the sound of a jet plane taking off. That night, I left the venue with my ears ringing and it took more than a week for the ringing to diminish. But after that, I thought no more of it.

That is, until I was in my mid-20s. I was working in a busy store with background noise from shoppers and music, and I started finding it difficult to hear what customers were saying. At home, my husband began to notice that I was either mishearing or not hearing things at all. On one occasion when we were at a noisy party, I had no idea what someone was saying to me, but I was nodding and smiling as if I understood. Afterward, my husband informed me that the person had been telling me that her dog had just died. Needless to say, I was extremely embarrassed. The result of this episode was that I went to see my GP to have my hearing checked.

The news was not good. I had hearing loss of 50 percent. It affected the top range of my hearing, which meant that any high-pitched noises, speech, phones, and day-to-day sounds were gone. I also had tinnitus, which was causing an infuriating ringing in my ears. The doctors explained that years of listening to loud music had caused the tiny sensory hair cells in the inner ear to become irreversibly flattened – meaning I would never hear properly again. And unless I protected my ears, my hearing would deteriorate even more.

So it turns out that my mother was right and I have, indeed, ruined my hearing. Today, I wear a pair of hearing aids that are very discreet but still definitely very uncool. But according to the World Health Organization, I am not alone. They say that around 26 million Americans risk serious damage to their ears by exposure to loud music. Hours spent listening to music on MP3 players and at concerts are to blame.

There are so many things that can be done to protect our hearing and it is often a case of "it'll never happen to me" or thinking that "only old people go deaf." However, in our modern life, where most people spend half their time plugged into a music device, it is very likely that it may, indeed, happen to you.

2 GRAMMAR gerunds and infinitives

a Circle the correct form.

1 We would like *paying* / *to pay* / *pay* our bill now because we're leaving early tomorrow.

2 My husband doesn't mind *doing* / *to do* / *do* housework.

3 I should *listening* / *to listen* / *listen* to some of their songs before I go to the concert.

4 Our teacher makes us *checking* / *to check* / *check* our homework.

5 Tom's doctor suggested *seeing* / *to see* / *see* a specialist about his back.

6 Mark learned *playing* / *to play* / *play* the guitar when he was a teenager.

7 My wife is very possessive. She doesn't let me *going out* / *to go out* / *go out* with my friends anymore.

8 The man denied *stealing* / *to steal* / *steal* the laptop from my bag.

9 Kim expects *getting* / *to get* / *get* her test scores on Friday.

10 I've given up *buying* / *to buy* / *buy* CDs because it's cheaper to download the tracks I like.

11 I can't imagine *having to* / *to have to* / *have to* get up at 6:00 every morning.

12 He managed *passing* / *to pass* / *pass* his driver's test even though he was really nervous.

b Complete the sentences with the correct form of a verb from the box.

buy   call   climb   ~~find~~
iron   read   send   spend

1 My sister is trying _to find_ a new job. She doesn't get along with her boss.

2 Do you remember _____ the apple tree in our parents' yard when we were children?

3 We need_____ a plumber because the shower's broken.

4 Laura forgot _____ her mother a birthday card.

5 I remembered _____ the milk, but I forgot to buy some bread!

6 If you can't sleep at night, try _____ a book in bed. It will help you relax.

7 That shirt needs _____ if you want to wear it tonight.

8 I'll never forget _____ a romantic weekend in Paris with my husband when we were first married.

3 VOCABULARY music

Clues across ➜

Clues down ⬇

4 PRONUNCIATION
words from other languages

a Circle the word with a different sound.

1 **k** keys	**ch**oir (**ch**urch) or**ch**estra psy**ch**ology	
2 **tʃ** chess	cappu**cc**ino **c**ello con**c**erto ma**cc**hiato	
3 **ʃ** shower	**ch**auffeur **ch**ef **ch**ic **ch**orus	
4 **k** keys	bou**qu**et en**c**ore fian**c**é hypo**ch**ondriac	

b ONLINE Listen and check. Then listen and repeat the words.

c ONLINE Listen and complete the sentences.

1 A lot of _paparazzi_ took _____ of the movie star.
2 The _____ is ruined by the _____ .
3 The _____ brought me my _____ .
4 The technician gave the _____ a new _____ .
5 The dancers in that _____ had a natural sense of _____ .

d Listen and check. Then listen and repeat the sentences.

USEFUL WORDS AND PHRASES

Learn these words and phrases.

be moved to tears /bi muvd tə tɪrz/
cacophony /kəˈkɑfəni/
deaf /dɛf/
make a fool of yourself /meɪk ə ful əv yərˈsɛlf/
musical genre /ˈmyuzɪkl ˈʒɑnrə/
nostalgia /nəˈstældʒə/
piece of music /pis əv ˈmyuzɪk/
profoundly /prəˈfaʊndli/
solo artist /ˈsoʊloʊ ˈɑrtɪst/
weep /wip/

---

5 LISTENING

a ONLINE Listen to a critic talking about a documentary film. What is the film mainly about?

A It tells the story of a man who suffers from Alzheimer's disease.
B It explains the different phases an Alzheimer's patient experiences.
C It describes a new treatment for Alzheimer's patients.

b Listen again and choose the right answer.

1 In his job, Dan Cohen is…
   a a filmmaker.
   b a musician.
   c a social worker.
2 Cohen creates the playlists for Alzheimer's patients to help them…
   a feel happier.
   b communicate better with their families.
   c recover some of their memories.
3 The first time Henry listens to his playlist, he…
   a is transformed.
   b starts crying.
   c starts dancing.
4 When the patients are wearing their headphones, they…
   a don't talk to anybody else.
   b are much more sociable.
   c don't take any notice of the staff members.
5 Dan Cohen wants other people to help him by…
   a creating playlists for old people.
   b giving money to the city's nursing homes.
   c giving the project devices that they no longer use.

c Listen again with the audio script on p.73 and try to guess the meaning of any words that you don't know. Then check in your dictionary.

Laugh and the world laughs with you, snore and you sleep alone.

Anthony Burgess, British writer

6B Sleeping Beauty

1 GRAMMAR

used to, be used to, get used to

a ⊙Circle the correct answer.

1 Before my sister had children she used to *sleep* / *sleeping* for eight hours every night.

2 When we moved to the US from Japan we weren't used to *drive* / *driving* on the right.

3 Chris got divorced last year, but he soon got used to *live* / *living* on his own.

4 I *used to* / *use to* know her, but we lost touch years ago.

5 My parents are slowly getting used to *be* / *being* retired.

6 My new job is exhausting. I'm not used to *work* / *working* so hard.

7 Did you use to *play* / *playing* a musical instrument at school?

8 When Bill was a student, he *used to* / *was used to* eat pizza every day.

b Rewrite the sentences using a form of *used to*, *get used to*, or *be used to* and a verb.

1 Stephen wasn't so assertive in the past.
Stephen _*didn't use to be*_ so assertive.

2 Has working at night become less of a problem now?
Have you _____ at night?

3 I don't usually have breakfast so early.
I'm _____ breakfast so early.

4 Chloe wore her sister's clothes when she was a child.
Chloe _____ her sister's clothes when she was a child.

5 We have adapted to living in the mountains very quickly.
We have _____ in the mountains very quickly.

6 She usually takes care of people, so she will make an excellent nurse.
She is _____ people, so she will make an excellent nurse.

7 They still don't know how to use the new system – they keep making mistakes.
They haven't _____ the new system yet.

8 I couldn't sleep because I don't usually sleep on a sofa.
I couldn't sleep because I _____ on a sofa.

2 READING

a Read the article quickly. Does the couple feel the same way about Adam's sleep talking?

b Read the text again and complete it with the missing sentences. There is one extra sentence you do not need to use.

A Ironically, Adam has never eaten them in his life.

B Karen's blog, "Sleep Talkin' Man," has become an Internet hit in more than 50 countries.

C Instead of investing in earplugs, she records her husband's comments.

D He went there once as a child, but he doesn't remember it.

E He thinks that his sleep-talking might be some sort of therapeutic process, because he always wakes up fully refreshed and relaxed.

F Karen says that Adam doesn't talk every night, but when he does, it happens every 30 seconds or few minutes.

How to deal with a sleep-talking husband

Most women would find it infuriating to be woken up night after night by their husband talking in his sleep. But one woman has found an interesting way of dealing with the problem. ¹_____ And then she posts them on the Internet.

Thirty-six-year-old Karen Slavick Lennard is a web-products manager, and she's married to Adam, an advertising account director, also thirty-six. They live together in southwestern London. Karen first entered Adam's lines onto her laptop by hand, but now she uses a voice-activated recorder. "I find every single thing Adam says hilarious," she says, "I cannot believe what he comes out with, and neither can he. We laugh like crazy every morning." ²_____ Then he suddenly stops.

Adam talks about everything and anything in his sleep; from vampire penguins to zombie guinea pigs. Examples of the things he has said in a typical week include, from Tuesday night: "Pork chops are the most satisfying. Mmmmmmm. Dangle them from the ceiling." ³_____ And then on Sunday at 5 a.m., he mumbled:

c Look at the highlighted words and phrases in the text and try to figure out their meaning. Then match them to definitions 1–10.

1 sudden expressions of strong feeling _____

2 made upset _____

3 said quietly without opening the mouth properly _____

4 put a dead body in the ground _____

5 says something unexpectedly _____

6 hang freely _____

7 taking action to solve _____

8 behaving in a wild way, without any control _____

9 the ability to remember _____

10 completely ridiculous _____

Pork chops are the most satisfying. Mmmmmmm. Dangle them from the ceiling.

Shhhhhh. Shhhhhh. I'm telling you: your voice, my ears. A bad combination.

Don't leave the duck there. It's totally irresponsible.

Your mom's at the door. Bury me deep. Bury me deep.

"Your mom's at the door. Bury me deep. Bury me deep." Another of his most memorable comments is: "Shhhhhh. Shhhhhh. I'm telling you: your voice, my ears. A bad combination."

Adam was shocked when he first heard the strange statements recorded by his wife. "I have no recollection of the absurd things I say," he explains. "They are not things that I would ever say or that any normal person would ever say." At first, Adam was put out by the recordings and he refused to listen to them, but later he realized that they were fun. "It was just my subconscious fully uninhibited and without restraint," he says. ⁴_____ And both he and his wife look forward to listening to the tapes in the morning.

In fact, Karen and Adam are not the only ones who find Adam's outbursts entertaining. ⁵_____ The couple has now started selling T-shirts and bags printed with Adam's comments on the site. The most popular among them are products featuring this one: "Don't leave the duck there. It's totally irresponsible."

3 VOCABULARY sleep

a Complete the sentences with a word connected to sleep.

1 We were cold in bed, so we opened the closet to look for a bl_anket_.

2 I never ov_____ because I always set my alarm clock before I go to bed.

3 She has to wear earplugs at night because her husband sn_____.

4 I was feeling sl_____, so I went to bed.

5 My grandmother takes sl_____ p_____ to help her to sleep.

6 It's impossible to wake Matt up. He sleeps like a l_____.

7 Alex never drinks coffee after dinner because it k_____ him a_____.

8 I was so tired that I fell asleep as soon as my head hit the p_____.

b Match the words in the box to the definitions.

comforter   fast asleep   insomnia   jet-lagged
nap   nightmare   set   yawn

1 a thick cover that you sleep under _comforter_

2 a short sleep during the day _____

3 the condition of being unable to sleep _____

4 you do this to an alarm _____ (it)

5 a very bad dream _____

6 you feel like this when you fly, for example, from New York to London _____

7 you sometimes do this when you're tired or bored _____

8 you're in this state when you're unlikely to wake up soon _____

4 PRONUNCIATION

sentence stress and linking

a ONLINE Listen and repeat the sentences. Try to link the words and copy the rhythm.

1 We used to use blankets, but now we have a comforter.
2 I'm not used to taking a nap after lunch.
3 We soon got used to living in our new house.
4 I never used to have problems sleeping.
5 Terry is used to working at night.
6 She couldn't get used to living on her own.

b Write the words in the correct column.

~~alarm~~   asleep   blanket   fall   insomnia
jet-lagged   nap   nightmare   siesta   yawn

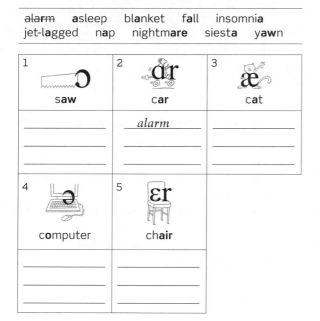

1 ɔ saw	2 ɑr car	3 æ cat
	alarm	

4 ə computer	5 ɛr chair

c ONLINE Listen and check. Then listen and repeat the words.

USEFUL WORDS AND PHRASES

Learn these words and phrases.

century /ˈsɛntʃəri/
deep sleep /dip slip/
nightfall /ˈnaɪtfɔl/
loyal /ˈlɔɪəl/
pray /preɪ/
sleepwalk /ˈslipwɔk/
syndrome /ˈsɪndroʊm/
video gamer /ˈvɪdioʊ ˈgeɪmər/
virtual reality /ˈvərtʃuəl riˈæləti/

---

5 LISTENING

a ONLINE Listen to a radio program about how diet affects sleep and choose the best answer.

The dietician gives advice about…in order to sleep well.
A what we should eat and drink
B what we shouldn't eat and drink
C what we should and shouldn't eat and drink

b Listen again and complete the notes.

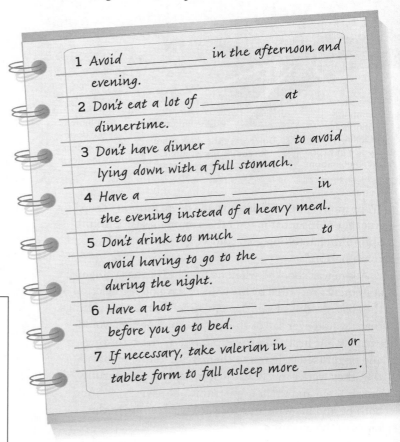

1 Avoid _____ in the afternoon and evening.
2 Don't eat a lot of _____ at dinnertime.
3 Don't have dinner _____ to avoid lying down with a full stomach.
4 Have a _____ _____ in the evening instead of a heavy meal.
5 Don't drink too much _____ to avoid having to go to the _____ during the night.
6 Have a hot _____ _____ before you go to bed.
7 If necessary, take valerian in _____ or tablet form to fall asleep more _____.

c Listen again with the audio script on p.73 and try to guess the meaning of any words that you don't know. Then check in your dictionary.

ONLINE **FILE 6**

7A Don't argue!

1 GRAMMAR past modals: *must have*, etc.

a Complete the sentences with *must have*, *might have*, or *couldn't have* and the verbs in parentheses.

1 You _must have been_ so happy when you passed your driver's test – it was your first time, wasn't it? (be)

2 I'm not sure where Mark is, but he _____ home. He wasn't feeling well earlier. (go)

3 You _____ my parents at the supermarket. They're away on vacation. (see)

4 I don't know why Ana hasn't arrived yet, but she _____ the wrong bus. (take)

5 The "For Sale" sign is still up outside their house. They _____ yet. (move)

6 Those boys look really guilty. They _____ something wrong. (do)

b Complete the sentences using *should* / *shouldn't* + a verb from the box.

buy	dress up	fill up	go off
leave	~~shout~~	stay up	take

1 My brother isn't talking to me. I _shouldn't have shouted_ at him.

2 We're running out of gas. We _____ _____ at the last gas station.

3 Someone took Ben's smartphone. He _____ it on his desk.

4 You won't be able to walk in those shoes. You _____ such high heels.

5 Jessie missed her train. She _____ a taxi to the station.

6 Your cousins look really scruffy. They _____ _____ for the wedding.

7 My alarm clock isn't working. It _____ _____ at seven thirty.

8 I had a nightmare last night. I _____ _____ to watch that horror movie.

c Complete the sentences with the words in the box. Use the past form of the modal verbs.

must / tell	~~might / leave~~	couldn't / be
may / fall	couldn't / see	must / forget
might / not / hear	may / not / have	

1 I wonder where my gloves are. I _might have left_ them in the car or maybe in the kitchen.

2 My father knew about the surprise party. Someone _____ him about it.

3 I don't understand how the accident happened. The driver _____ asleep.

4 Adam passed the exam without studying. It _____ very difficult.

5 I'm sure my grandmother was home, but she didn't answer the door. She _____ the doorbell.

6 When I got up this morning, the TV was still on in the living room. You _____ to turn it off.

7 The children didn't make their beds this morning. They _____ time.

8 **A** Your boyfriend walked past me without saying hello.

 B He _____ you.

43

2 READING

a Read the text quickly and answer the questions.

1 What is the problem with online arguments?

2 What does Professor Markman think is the solution?

Internet rage: a new trend?

Until now, people have usually conducted their arguments face-to-face. A disagreement occurs and each side wants to make his or her views known. But the Internet has changed all this. Today, more and more people are getting involved in arguments online. Many of these take place in the comments section that follows below articles on news websites. The tone of some of the posts on these threads can be extremely aggressive. So why is everyone so angry on the Internet?

Art Markman, a professor of psychology at the University of Texas, has an explanation for this. First, he points out that the people who post these comments are anonymous. Nobody knows their real name or who they are, which means that they do not have to explain their actions. Second, the commenter and the person who is the target of their anger are not actually in the same room. The distance between them makes the commenter lose his inhibitions, and so he becomes more offensive. Third, it is much easier to be nasty in writing than in speech, according to Professor Markman.

Although Professor Markman believes in self-expression, he regards online arguments as a complete waste of time. He says that the whole point of an argument is to try to persuade someone else to agree with you. In order to do this, the people involved have to listen to each other. This sort of interaction is lacking on the Internet, says Professor Markman. Exchanges on comment threads do not happen in real time and so people have longer to focus on their opinion and write lengthy monologues to justify themselves. In the process, they become even more convinced that they are right, and they stop listening to other people. In the end, there is a complete absence of communication and the only thing they have achieved is to work themselves up into a rage.

So, what is the solution? Professor Markman does not think that comment threads should be banned, but he does think that controls should be stricter. In his view, it is the news outlets themselves who should be responsible for the content of the thread. "If, on a website, comments are left up that are making personal attacks in the nastiest way, you're sending the message that this is acceptable human behavior," he says. Professor Markman would like site administrators to remove the offending remarks from the comment thread. "Having a conversation with someone you don't agree with is a skill," he says. Unfortunately, it seems to be a skill that some commenters are not familiar with.

b Read the text again and choose the right answers.

1 Arguments on the Internet occur most frequently when someone…

  a expresses an opinion in the wrong way.

  b has a negative opinion about a website.

  c disagrees with a comment about an article.

2 According to Professor Markman, arguments online are more aggressive than face-to-face arguments because the commenter…

  a lives in a different town or country.

  b doesn't disclose his or her identity.

  c is experienced in commenting on articles.

3 Professor Markman thinks that online arguments have no value because people tend to…

  a spend too long reading other people's views.

  b make too many mistakes in their comments.

  c ignore other people's opinions.

4 In Professor Markman's view, an online argument usually results in the participants…

  a feeling angry.

  b avoiding a particular website.

  c writing fewer comments in the future.

5 Professor Markman believes that news websites should…

  a stop allowing people to comment on their articles.

  b monitor comment threads more carefully.

  c prohibit certain people from posting comments.

c Look at the highlighted words and phrases in the text and try to figure out their meaning. Then use them to complete the sentences.

1 She had a particularly _nasty_ customer last week who made her cry.

2 I was the _____ of a lot of criticism after the article I wrote last month.

3 Since he retired, he has been _____ local politics.

4 When he was a child he used to work himself up into a _____ when he didn't get what he wanted.

5 I found your comment about my friend's appearance extremely _____.

6 The police will _____ any vehicles that are illegally parked.

7 I feel there is something _____ in my life.

8 Internet _____ are often dominated by a small number of angry people.

3 VOCABULARY verbs often confused

a Choose the correct verbs.

1 I *wish* / (*hope*) they'll accept my credit card because I don't have enough cash.

2 I don't *mind* / *matter* where we go. The important thing is to have a good time on vacation.

3 My daughter will do anything to *avoid* / *prevent* doing housework. She's really lazy.

4 *Remember* / *Remind* me to send my dad a card. It's his birthday next week.

5 My boyfriend and I often *argue* / *discuss* about his friends. I really don't like them.

6 Susan *looks* / *seems* really unhappy in her new job. She was telling me about it on the phone today.

7 I didn't *notice* / *realize* what the thief was wearing. It was too dark to see anything.

b Complete the sentences with the correct verb from each pair in the past simple.

advise / warn	beat / win	deny / refuse
expect / wait	lay / lie	raise / rise	rob / steal

1 The tour guide _warned_ us that the area was dangerous at night.

2 I _____ our team to lose, but in the end they won.

3 Canada _____ the US 3–2.

4 Somebody _____ me while I was asleep. They took my credit cards and all my money.

5 My colleague _____ taking the file, but I saw it later on his desk.

6 Last year we just _____ on the beach all day when we were on vacation.

7 House prices _____ last month for the first time this year.

4 MINI GRAMMAR *would rather*

Rewrite the sentences using *would rather*.

1 I'd prefer to sit by the window than next to the aisle.
   I'd rather sit by the window than next to the aisle.

2 What do you want to do, stay in or go out?
   _____

3 I don't really want to cook tonight if you don't mind.
   _____

4 Where do you want to go, Boston or New York?
   _____

5 I'd prefer to walk than take the car.
   _____

6 I don't really want to go to the movies if you don't mind.
   _____

5 PRONUNCIATION sentence stress

ONLINE Listen and repeat the second sentences. Copy the rhythm.

1 They're taking Steve to the hospital. He **might** have **broken** a **bone**.

2 Ella isn't here yet. She **couldn't** have **gotten** my **message**.

3 It was only a joke. She **shouldn't** have gotten so angry.

4 This restaurant is packed. We **should** have **made** a reservation.

5 I didn't hear the phone. I **must** have **been** asleep.

6 Becky and Ian aren't at the party. They **may** have **forgotten** about it.

6 LISTENING

a **ONLINE** Listen to five speakers talking about a time when they had an argument with someone. Where did the arguments start?

1 In the _____.
2 In the _____.
3 In the _____.
4 In the _____.
5 At _____.

b Listen again and write the number of the speaker in each box.

The argument finished when somebody…

A ☐ confirmed who was right.
B ☐ realized they had forgotten something.
C ☐ said something unrelated to the conversation.
D ☐ made a terrible mess.
E ☐ physically removed one of the people involved.

c Listen again with the audio script on p.74 and try to guess the meaning of any words that you don't know. Then check in your dictionary.

USEFUL WORDS AND PHRASES

Learn these words and phrases.

avoid confrontation /əˈvɔɪd kɑnfrənˈteɪʃn/

back up (an argument) /bæk ʌp/

bother (v) /ˈbɑðər/

bring up (a topic of conversation) /brɪŋ ʌp/

blame (somebody for doing something) /bleɪm/

change the subject /tʃeɪndʒ ðə ˈsʌbdʒɛkt/

insult (somebody) /ɪnˈsʌlt/

insult (noun) /ˈɪnsʌlt/

threaten /ˈθrɛtn/

swear word /ˈswɛr wərd/

With any part you play, there is a certain amount of yourself in it.
There has to be, otherwise it's just not acting. It's lying.

Johnny Depp, American actor

7B Actors acting

1 GRAMMAR
verbs of the senses

a Circle the correct form.

1 Your skin *feels* / *feels like* dry. You need to use some hand cream.

2 Ken's sweating. He *looks* / *looks as if* he's been running.

3 We need to take out the trash. The kitchen *smells* / *smells like* terrible.

4 I'm not sure what's in this curry but it *tastes like* / *tastes as if* chicken.

5 I think this bag is real leather. It *feels like* / *feels as if* leather anyway.

6 It *sounds* / *sounds as if* Tina has finally gotten up. I can hear her moving around.

7 This soup *tastes* / *tastes as if* you used sugar instead of salt.

b Complete the sentences with a verb of the senses + *like* or *as if* where necessary.

1 A lot of singers today ___sound___ exactly the same.

2 This salad _____ horrible – it's really salty.

3 Your boyfriend _____ a police officer – he's tall and well built.

4 Have you turned off the stove? It _____ something is burning.

5 What's that noise? It _____ thunder.

6 My skin _____ much softer since I've been using a new face cream.

7 Martha's hair is a mess. She _____ she just got out of bed.

2 VOCABULARY the body

a Complete the puzzle to find the hidden body part.

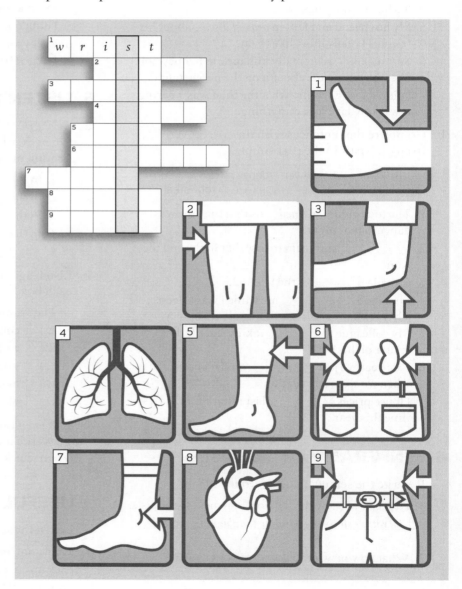

b Circle the correct answer.

1 My boyfriend *eats* / *bites* his nails when he's nervous.

2 You must be tired because you can't stop *scratching* / *yawning*.

3 John went into the room and *shook* / *winked* hands with the interviewer.

4 She *waved* / *frowned* at me from the other side of the street to get my attention.

5 Kayla *clapped* / *combed* her hair and put on her jacket to go out.

6 I hate it when people *stare* / *raise* at me when I am on a bus or on the subway.

3 READING

a Read the article quickly and choose the right answer.

What kind of clues does the article say can enable us to spot a liar?
a verbal clues
b nonverbal clues
c both verbal and nonverbal clues

b Read the article again and mark the sentences **T** (true) or **F** (false).

1 White lies are less serious than other lies. ____
2 Ordinary people are conscious of just over half of the lies they are told. ____
3 People who are lying cannot keep still. ____
4 Liars are incapable of maintaining eye contact. ____
5 It is easy to smile, even when you don't feel like it. ____
6 You can detect a real smile because of the lines around the mouth. ____
7 People will know that you are lying if you shake your head when you say yes. ____
8 Liars never shrug their shoulders when they are telling you a story. ____
9 People only use one side of their face to show contempt. ____
10 As soon as you spot a person making one of the signs, you know that they are lying. ____

c Look at the highlighted words and phrases in the text and try to figure out their meaning. Then use them to complete the sentences.

1 It is a popular _____ that we only use 10 % of our brains.
2 I _____ you won't be going to the party now that you know your ex-wife will be there.
3 She lit a candle to try to _____ the smell of smoke in the room.
4 That watch must be a _____. You can't get a Rolex for that price!
5 I sometimes tell my wife _____ to avoid arguments.
6 Little children tend to _____. Sometimes, they just can't keep still.
7 We'll know soon if those boys broke the window or not. Their guilty faces will _____.
8 They are examining the document to see if it is _____.

How to spot **a liar**

People tell us lies every single day. Some of these lies are white lies, told to protect our social dignity or to keep a secret that needs to be kept. But others are more dangerous and can cause serious problems. According to Pamela Meyer in her best-selling book *Liespotters*, most of us only realize that someone is lying to us 54 % of the time. In her book, Ms. Meyer explains the patterns used to recognize deception by liespotters like herself.

Ms. Meyer starts by disproving some of the myths about liars and their body language. For example, most people believe that liars tend to move around and fidget a lot when they are not telling the truth. In fact, people tend to freeze their upper bodies when they are lying, she says. Another misconception is that liars will not look a person in the eye. According to Ms. Meyer, they maintain eye contact a little too much because they have already heard about the myth. In general, liars are very good actors, but one thing that can give them away is their smile.

In her book, Ms. Meyer explains how it is possible to detect a fake smile. Smiling is a conscious action, she says, and anybody can do it just by contracting the muscles in their cheeks. The secret to a real smile lies in the eyes. We have some lines at the outer corner of our eyes called crow's feet, which appear when we give a genuine smile. It is impossible to consciously contract the muscles around the eyes to produce these lines. This means that a smile that doesn't reach the eyes is not real.

Further signs that give liars away, according to Ms. Meyer, are differences between their words and their actions. Someone who shakes their head when they are saying "yes" is lying, as is a person who shrugs their shoulders when they are trying to tell a convincing story. Facial expressions are another clue. Liars are experts at faking expressions for long periods of time in order to mask what they really feel. Often, the emotion they are trying to hide suddenly appears on their face for a second. Ms. Meyer identifies the worst of these emotions as contempt: a feeling that a person is without value. Contempt is shown by pulling one corner of the lips up and in.

Ms. Meyer warns us, however, that we shouldn't presume that somebody is lying just because we have seen *one* of the signs. But we should be suspicious when we see many of the signs together. When we spot that we're being lied to, our next job is to find out the truth, and that requires completely different skills.

4 MINI GRAMMAR *as*

Match the sentence halves.

1 I'm not as assertive   `d`
2 My brother works as   ☐
3 As we were boarding the plane   ☐
4 Today is just as hot   ☐
5 On the picnic we used a sheet as   ☐
6 As the actors came back on stage   ☐

a the audience started to clap.
b as yesterday.
c a tablecloth.
d as my sister.
e an educational psychologist.
f I dropped my passport.

5 PRONUNCIATION silent letters

Cross out the silent consonants in these words.
Use the phonetics to help you.

1 w̶rist   /rɪst/
2 thumb   /θʌm/
3 kneel   /nil/
4 palm   /pɑm/
5 muscle   /ˈmʌsl/
6 whistle   /ˈwɪsl/

USEFUL WORDS AND PHRASES

Learn these words and phrases.

achieve (something) /əˈtʃiv/
body language /ˈbɑdi læŋgwɪdʒ/
break (something) open /breɪk ˈoʊpən/
in contrast /ɪn ˈkɑntræst/
pursue /pərˈsu/
spot (something) /spɑt/
suspicion /səˈspɪʃn/
telltale sign /ˈtɛlteɪl saɪn/

---

6 LISTENING

a **ONLINE** Listen to a radio program about acting. According to the program, what two things do the actors below have in common?

1 _____
2 _____

Daniel Day-Lewis   Charlize Theron

b Listen again and choose the right answer.

1 Method actors are able to reproduce the…of their characters.
   a appearance   b emotions   c voices

2 A sense memory is the recollection of…from the past.
   a events   b feelings   c experiences

3 Actors do sense memory exercises…
   a for short periods.
   b for long periods on several days.
   c for one long period.

4 Unlike method actors, ordinary actors use their… when they perform.
   a minds   b minds and bodies   c bodies

5 Actor Daniel Day-Lewis…before filming starts.
   a lives like his character
   b meets his character
   c writes about his character

6 People were so impressed by Charlize Theron in *Monster* because…
   a she lost a lot of weight for the part.
   b she looked incredibly attractive on the screen.
   c she was capable of playing a completely different role.

c Listen again with the audio script on p.74 and try to guess the meaning of any words that you don't know. Then check in your dictionary.

Colloquial English Talking about... acting

1 LOOKING AT LANGUAGE

Complete the modifiers in the sentences.

1 The actors were utt*erly* exhausted when the play was over.
2 The plot left the audience feeling com_____ bewildered.
3 As far as I'm concerned, the movie was tre_____ overrated.
4 So far, reviews of the play have been over_____ positive.
5 Mozart was an extra_____ talented musician.
6 The director was ab_____ delighted to receive the award.
7 All of the characters were wearing fan_____ original costumes.

2 READING

a Read the biographical information about Peter Shaffer.
Then read the article about how *Amadeus* was made and choose the correct answers.

1 What was it about Mozart that appealed to Peter Shaffer?
   a The opposing sides of his character.
   b His outstanding talent as a musician.
   c His lack of maturity.
   d His relationship with his family and friends.
2 Why did Peter Shaffer ask Peter Hall to direct *Amadeus*?
   a Because he was one of Shaffer's best friends.
   b Because he was the director of a prestigious theater.
   c Because he had more directing experience than Dexter.
   d Because he knew a lot about the operas of the main character in the play.
3 Who had doubts about Simon Callow's ability to play the leading role?
   a Peter Shaffer
   b John Dexter
   c Simon Callow
   d Peter Hall
4 What did Peter Shaffer do while the cast was rehearsing?
   a He made sure that the actors didn't laugh.
   b He adapted some of his original ideas.
   c He checked that the actors were following the script.
   d He made a note of any problems that came up.
5 What was the initial reaction to the play?
   a Everybody loved it.
   b Its reception was mixed.
   c Most people were very angry about it.
   d Nobody liked it.

b Look at the highlighted words and phrases. What do you think they mean? Use your dictionary to look up their meaning and pronunciation.

THE MAKING OF *Amadeus*

The play *Amadeus* was written by the English playwright Peter Shaffer. He came up with the idea after reading extensively about the composer Wolfgang Amadeus Mozart. In the course of his reading, he was struck by the contrast between the quality of Mozart's music, which was obviously the work of a genius, and the silliness of his letters written to his family and friends, which could have been written by an eight-year-old. The tone of the letters was often rather vulgar.

Once his play was complete, Shaffer had to decide on a director. The experienced director John Dexter had previously directed three of Shaffer's plays, so he was the obvious choice. However, the two had an argument about financial issues, so Shaffer had to find an alternative. During a conversation with Peter Hall, the director of the Royal National Theatre, Hall told Shaffer how much he longed to direct *Amadeus*. Having directed productions of most of Mozart's operas, Shaffer decided that he was the ideal person for the job.

Before his quarrel with Shaffer, Dexter had already cast Simon Callow, then a young unknown actor, as Mozart. In the period between directors, Callow had started having doubts about his role. He told Shaffer that he didn't think he was the right person to play the composer. Shaffer, however, trusted Dexter's judgment even though he had no idea then about Callow's talents. He reassured Callow, who eventually agreed to go ahead with the role.

Rehearsals for the play started badly. At first, when Callow said his lines, the cast got the giggles because the language was so childish and vulgar. But then, the playwright and director got the actors together to discuss the childishness behind Mozart's genius, and they began to understand what the play was trying to say. From then on, the actors were impatient for rehearsals to start each day. While they were rehearsing, Shaffer sat in a theater seat, rewriting some of the scenes. According to the playwright, rehearsals were a joy to watch and both director and actors now felt confident that the play would become a theater classic.

On the opening night, Peter Shaffer was criticized by some members of the audience for portraying Mozart as an imbecile. Others, however, praised the way in which the playwright had chosen to show both sides of the composer's personality. They realized that the vulgarity was meant to highlight Mozart's humanity in contrast to his genius. Despite the controversy, *Amadeus* was a great success, and it won the 1981 Tony Award for Best Play. The play was later adapted by Shaffer for the 1984 Academy Award-winning movie of the same name.

Glossary
John Dexter a leading English director of opera and theater (1925–1990)
Peter Hall an English theater and movie director, director of the Royal National Theatre from 1973 to 1988 (1930–)

No one truly knows a nation until one has been inside its jails.

Nelson Mandela

8A Beat the robbers...and the burglars

1 VOCABULARY crime and punishment

a Order the letters to make words for crimes.

1 gbrryual   _burglary_
2 jkihigcan   _____
3 gsunimlgg   _____
4 gorrfey   _____
5 lsivdnaam   _____
6 rudaf   _____
7 bbrriey   _____
8 drmeur   _____

b Complete the chart.

Crime	Criminal	Verb
kidnapping	*kidnapper*	*to kidnap*
	blackmailer	
		to sell drugs
mugging		
		to set off bombs
		to steal
robbery		
	stalker	
		to hack

c Complete the sentences with the correct form of a word from **a** or **b**.

1 The _kidnapper_ took the child while she was playing outside her house.
2 Fortunately there were no customers in the bank when the _____ happened.
3 The _____ followed the actress everywhere she went.
4 They were trying to _____ electronic goods into the country, but they were caught at customs.
5 The mayor accepted a _____ in exchange for allowing the company to build on that land.
6 Two men _____ my friend while she was at the ATM yesterday. They took all her money.
7 Someone managed to _____ into her computer and find her personal information.
8 A _____ broke into my house while I was away and stole my laptop.

d Circle the correct word.

1 A man has been *caught* | *arrested* in connection with the robbery at the bank yesterday.
2 It took the jury two weeks to reach their *punishment* | *verdict* of "not guilty."
3 The victim's husband has been *charged* | *committed* with the murder of his wife.
4 The criminal will appear in *court* | *judge* next week.
5 Police are *investigating* | *questioning* the kidnapping of a millionaire's son in Los Angeles.
6 The judge *acquitted* | *sentenced* the accused man because there was no evidence.
7 The *jury* | *witnesses* who had seen the burglary reported it to the police.
8 He got a $300 *fine* | *sentence* for illegal parking.

2 READING

a Read the article and answer the questions with the paragraph letter.

In which technique…

1 does the victim put himself in danger by downloading files from the Internet? ___
2 is the victim tricked into replying to an email? ___
3 does the thief look through the victim's things with his own hands? ___
4 is the victim tricked into making a phone call? ___
5 is the thief in control of the victim's electronic device? ___
6 does the thief speak to the victim personally? ___

b Look at the highlighted words and phrases in the text and try to figure out their meaning. Then use them to complete the sentences.

1 Please _____ your name and email address.
2 I have your cell phone number, but I don't have your _____ .
3 You can _____ any of these items at our online store.
4 If you _____ room service, please press 1.
5 Remember to use a shredder when you _____ any envelopes or letters that contain your personal information.
6 With digital TV, you _____ hundreds of different channels.
7 The police have asked for more time to _____ evidence.
8 Tomorrow I'm going to _____ my closet and throw away all my old clothes.

Top techniques in identity theft

Identity theft is the illegal use of somebody else's personal information in order to obtain money or credit. Victims of identity theft can face financial and even legal problems in the future because an impostor has used their personal information to purchase something or give false information to the authorities. The best way of preventing thieves from stealing your identity is to know how they operate. Here are some of the most common identity theft techniques.

A Phishing

You get an email that claims to be from a financial institution or other business asking for some personal information from you. It contains a link to a web page where you have to key in your bank username and password. The new page may look real but it is, in fact, a fake. Identity thieves will take all of the information you give on the page and use it to steal money from your accounts.

B Smishing

You get a text message that seems to require your immediate attention, for example: "[Name of bank] confirms that you have bought a computer from [Name of retailer]. Call [Phone Number] if you have not made this purchase." When you call the number, an automated voice response system asks you to confirm your credit card details. The text message is actually from a group of identity thieves who can create and use a duplicate bank card within 30 minutes of obtaining the necessary information.

C Vishing

This occurs when you receive a phone call on your landline from someone who seems to be trying to help you. The person claims to have detected fraudulent activity on your credit card and asks you to confirm your credit card details. The call is actually from an identity thief who wants to use your card to purchase things for himself.

D Spoofing

Hackers break into your computer and transfer communication from a legitimate website to a fake one. For example, when you try to log into Facebook, your computer will take you to the hacker's site, where they will steal your log-in information. From there, they will have access to plenty of details, such as your date of birth and the names of the members of your family. Later, they can use this information to steal your identity.

E Spyware

Spyware is a type of software used on the Internet to gather information about a person or organization without their consent. Identity thieves often attach it to downloadable files, such as online games. When you install the game, a hacker records all your keystrokes, including things like credit card numbers or bank account logins.

F Digging through your trash can

The trash can be a great source of personal information and in some cases, identity thieves actually go through the garbage to see what they can find. Make sure you completely destroy your old credit cards when it is time to dispose of them. As far as official documents are concerned, you should put them all through a shredder or burn them before you throw them out.

3 GRAMMAR passive (all forms); *it is said that..., he is thought to...,* etc.

a Complete the text with the correct active or passive form of the verb in parentheses.

As a police officer, I was very upset when my motorcycle [1] _was taken_ (take) from outside my house last month. When I found out that over 20 motorcycles [2] _____ (steal) in my area in the previous six months, I promised myself that the thief would [3] _____ (catch) and [4] _____ (punish). First, my colleagues and I [5] _____ (question) all the victims of the thefts and [6] _____ (visit) all the motorcycle dealers in the area. Our investigations came to an end late last night when we identified the criminal... as my next-door neighbor!

He [7] _____ (just arrest) and right now he [8] _____ (hold) at the local police station. His case [9] _____ (hear) in the County Courthouse next week, and we all [10] _____ (expect) him to be found guilty. He might [11] _____ (give) a short prison sentence, but the best thing is that no more motorcycles [12] _____ (steal) in my area in the near future.

b Rewrite the sentences.

1 It is known that the drug dealer is a local man.
   The drug dealer is known to be a local man .

2 The blackmailer is understood to be a colleague of the victim.
   It is understood that the blackmailer is a colleague of the victim .

3 It is expected that the man will be acquitted.
   The man _____ .

4 It is reported that kidnappers have taken the president's wife.
   Kidnappers _____ .

5 The terrorists are thought to be in hiding somewhere in France.
   It is _____ .

6 The suspect is known to be dangerous.
   It is _____ .

7 It is reported that vandals have damaged the art gallery.
   Vandals _____ .

8 The police are said to have arrested three men.
   It is _____ .

4 MINI GRAMMAR *have something done*

Rewrite the sentences with *have something done*.

1 Someone is going to change the lock on my front door.
   I'm going to _have the lock on my front door changed_.
2 Someone tests our burglar alarm twice a year.
   We _____ twice a year.
3 A mechanic has repaired my car.
   I _____.
4 Someone painted my brother's house.
   My brother _____.
5 Someone will clean my rugs in the spring.
   I _____ in the spring.
6 Some men are building a wall around my neighbor's yard.
   My neighbors _____ around their yard.
7 Someone cleans Oliver's apartment once a week.
   Oliver _____ once a week.
8 A company is redesigning our kitchen.
   We _____.

5 PRONUNCIATION the letter *u*

a (Circle) the word with a different sound.

1 ɜr **bird**	burglar murderer (secure) verdict
2 ∧ **up**	judge jury drugs punishment
3 ɔ **saw**	caught guilty stalker fraud
4 aɪ **bike**	trial bribery blackmail hijack

b **ONLINE** Listen and check. Then listen and repeat the words.

6 LISTENING

a **ONLINE** Listen to five people talking about different crimes and write speaker 1–5 next to each sentence. There is one sentence you do not need to use.

A The victim was congratulated by local people. ___
B The victim was hurt during the incident. ___
C The victim was lucky because the police saw the incident. ___
D The victim and other people were too surprised to react. ___
E The victim recovered one of the stolen belongings. ___
F The victim has experienced the same crime more than once. ___

b Listen again and mark the sentences **T** (true) or **F** (false).

1 Speaker 1 was walking to work when the incident happened. ___
2 Speaker 2 takes precautions to avoid having things stolen. ___
3 Speaker 3 was robbed because he / she was not paying attention. ___
4 Speaker 4 was alone when the incident happened. ___
5 Speaker 5 was shopping when he / she witnessed a crime. ___

c Listen again with the audio script on p.75 and try to guess the meaning of any words that you don't know. Then check in your dictionary.

USEFUL WORDS AND PHRASES

Learn these words and phrases.

against the law /əˈgɛnst ðə lɔ/
cab (= taxi) /kæb/
download music (from the Internet) /ˈdaʊnloʊd ˈmyuzɪk/
false identity /fɔls aɪˈdɛntəti/
hesitate /ˈhɛzəteɪt/
ignore /ɪgˈnɔr/
illegal /ɪˈligl/
make eye contact /meɪk aɪ ˈkɑntækt/
overprotective /oʊvərprəˈtɛktɪv/
suspicious /səˈspɪʃəs/
Watch out! /wɑtʃ aʊt/

A newspaper is a device unable to discriminate between
a bicycle accident and the collapse of civilization.
George Bernard Shaw, Irish author and playwright

8B Breaking news

1 GRAMMAR reporting verbs

a Complete with the gerund or the infinitive of the verb in parentheses.

1 The girl refused _to dance_ with my friend. (dance)
2 My husband denied _____ the last piece of cake. (eat)
3 My parents told me _____ late. (not be)
4 The tour guide recommended _____ the Picasso Museum. (visit)
5 I agreed _____ in front of my neighbor's garage. (not park)
6 The police accused him of _____ them the truth. (not tell)
7 My boyfriend asked me _____ him to the train station. (take)
8 The teacher threatened _____ them extra homework if they didn't stop talking. (give)
9 Jane promised _____ my book the next day. (return)
10 The woman admitted _____ the man's watch. (steal)

b Report the direct speech using one of the reporting verbs from the box.

| advise | apologize | insist | invite |
| offer | remind | suggest | warn |

1 "Don't forget to sign the documents," my boss told me.
My boss _reminded me to sign_ the documents.
2 "I really don't think you should leave your job," Jack's friend told him.
Jack's friend _____ his job.
3 "Why don't we go for a walk?" said Katie.
Katie _____ for a walk.
4 "I'll make lunch," her husband said.
Her husband _____ lunch.
5 "Don't park on this street," the man said to us.
The man _____ there.
6 "I'm sorry I was so rude," I said.
I _____ so rude.
7 "Would you like to have dinner with me?" Andy asked Sarah.
Andy _____ with him.
8 "I'm going with you to the doctor's," Alice said to me.
Alice _____ to the doctor's with me.

2 VOCABULARY the media

a Complete the sentences with jobs in the media.

1 The p*aparazzi* were waiting outside the restaurant to photograph the movie star.
2 I'm surprised none of the cr_ _ _ _ _ liked the movie; I thought it was great!
3 The n_ _ _ _ _ _ _ _ _ _ was very embarrassed when he couldn't pronounce the politician's name.
4 The sports c_ _ _ _ _ _ _ _ _ _ got very excited when the first goal was scored.
5 My brother is a r_ _ _ _ _ _ _ for *The Sunday Times*.
6 The newspaper e_ _ _ _ _ decided not to print the reporter's story because it was too politically sensitive.
7 I stopped watching that show because I can't stand the news a_ _ _ _ _.
8 Laura works from home as a fr_ _ _ _ _ _ _ j_ _ _ _ _ _ _ _ _.
9 Have you ever written an email to an a_ _ _ _ _ c_ _ _ _ _ _ _ _ asking for advice?

b Complete the headlines with a word from the box.

| back | bids | clash | hit | quit | quiz | spat | split | tabbed | wed |

1 **TV host axed by ABC in** _spat_ **over dress code.**
2 Singer to _____ Brazilian model.
3 **Senator to _____ after revelations about personal life.**
4 Police _____ wife after man disappears.
5 Hollywood stars _____ presidential candidate.
6 **US stock market _____ by new company scandal.**
7 Ex-basketball player _____ to win reality show.
8 Supermarket _____ to attract customers by slashing prices.
9 **Players _____ over referee's decision.**
10 Celebrity couple _____ after five years.

3 READING

a Read the article and complete it with the missing headings.

   A **Visit different places**
   B **You are paid to read**
   C **No two days are ever the same**
   D **You can see your name in print**
   E **You're always finding out new things**
   F **You can be an opinion maker**
   G **You meet all kinds of people**
   H **Every minute counts**

b Find the words or phrases in the text to match definitions 1–9.

1 deal with something (*introduction*) _____
2 about twelve (*paragraph 1*) _____
3 more intelligent (*paragraph 2*) _____
4 sometimes (*paragraph 3*) _____
5 an increase in your salary (*paragraph 4*) _____
6 remain in control of (*paragraph 5*) _____
7 a time or date before which something must be finished (*paragraph 6*) _____
8 repeated exactly as it was written (*paragraph 7*) _____
9 a strong need or desire (*paragraph 8*) _____

Journalism:
the best job ever

Not everyone can handle a career in journalism – it can be stressful and the hours are long – but it's a fantastic, and popular, career choice. Here are eight reasons why.

1 ____
The first thing you do to start your working day is sit down and find out what's been happening in the world since you went to sleep the night before. Reading a dozen or so news outlets and blogs with your morning coffee is a better way to start the day than sitting in traffic in the rush hour!

2 ____
When you start writing a new story, you know nothing, or very little, about it. But by the time you hand your finished article to the editor, you're an expert on that story. You're constantly learning and getting smarter when you're a journalist.

3 ____
On a single day, you could be at your desk researching some new story. Or you might cover a press event with a photographer, or interview a contact for a developing story. From time to time you might even be asked to review a restaurant or cultural event. You never know what the day is going to bring.

4 ____
One of the highlights of the job is interviewing really interesting people you wouldn't usually have the chance to talk to: from "ordinary" people who have done something extraordinary, to sportspeople, artists, and musicians. And you don't have to worry about what you say to everyone you meet, either – if you ask a politician a question they don't like, you could get a pay raise.

5 ____
It's a big, fast world, and it's important to be where the news is happening, particularly with events that have a global significance like conflicts or protests. Not all journalists travel a lot, but many do. Situations change quickly these days and it's important to stay on top of the story.

6 ____
A newsroom is a fast-paced environment and a journalist works on a tight deadline, so there's always a certain adrenaline rush. If you are the type of person who works best under pressure, it's the best job ever.

7 ____
It's a great feeling to have your name on a published article, or to have something you've written quoted in another article. And when someone tells you that they've read your article and they like what you've written, that's even better.

8 ____
If you have an urge to write and you are curious about the world around you, a career in journalism is the obvious choice. The best journalists are the ones who really try to understand every aspect of a story, and then explain that story well. A good, well-written article can influence the way people think.

4 PRONUNCIATION word stress

a Write the reporting verbs in the correct column.

a|ccuse ad|mit ad|vise a|gree
con|vince de|ny in|sist in|vite
o|ffer per|suade pro|mise re|fuse
re|mind sug|gest threa|ten

b **ONLINE** Listen and check. Then listen and repeat the reporting verbs.

stress on 1st syllable		stress on 2nd syllable	
		accuse	

5 LISTENING

a **ONLINE** Listen to an extract from a program about a famous mistake on TV. Answer the questions.

1 During which program did the mistake occur?
_____

2 In which year did the mistake occur? _____

3 Who is Michael Fish? _____

4 What did the woman ask about when she called?
_____

5 What was Michael's answer?
_____

6 How strong were the worst winds?
_____

7 How many people died in the storm?
_____

8 How many trees fell down? _____

9 Where did Michael Fish appear in 2012?
_____

10 Where can you see the original weather broadcast made by Michael Fish? _____

WITH MICHAEL FISH

b Listen again with the audio script on p.75 and try to guess the meaning of any words that you don't know. Then check in your dictionary.

USEFUL WORDS AND PHRASES

Learn these words and phrases.

celebrity gossip /səˈlɛbrəti ˈɡɑsəp/
censorship /ˈsɛnsərˌʃɪp/
skip (a section of the newspaper) /skɪp/

sports scores /spɔrts skɔrz/
the latest news /ðə ˈleɪtəst nuz/
the media /ðə ˈmidiə/

print newspaper /prɪnt ˈnuzpeɪpər/
online newspaper /ɑnˈlaɪn ˈnuzpeɪpər/
private life /ˈpraɪvət laɪf/

> No man has a good enough memory to be a successful liar.
>
> *Abraham Lincoln, US President*

1 READING

a Read the article about Ponzi schemes quickly and match the years to the people.

2009	Charles Ponzi
2008	Early Ponzi schemers
1920s	Lou Pearlman
1880s	Bernard Madoff

b Read the text again and complete it with the missing sentences. There is one extra sentence you do not need to use.

A He continued to happily take money from excited new investors on a daily basis, many of whom gave him their life savings.

B If you don't believe him, just ask your friends.

C He was able to convince them because he was a highly respected and well-established financial expert.

D Among the fake companies he created was an airline, which existed solely on paper.

E The whole thing collapsed and the authorities caught him.

F However, the scheme doesn't work for long because of the constant need to find new investors.

c Look at the highlighted words and phrases in the text and try to figure out their meaning. Then match them to definitions 1–7.

1 can be relied on to be good, honest, and responsible _____

2 coming in great numbers

_____

3 pay for _____

4 collapses, stops working

_____

5 a voucher that can be exchanged for cash

6 another word for an American dollar

_____

7 allowed and acceptable according to the law _____

Ponzi schemes

Want to know an easy route onto the world's rich list? You may think it's an impossible dream, but as Charles Ponzi reveals, all you really need is a persuasive smile and the ability to lie very, very well.

The man behind the name

Charles Ponzi was an Italian immigrant living in the United States who cheated countless innocent people out of money in the 1920s. At that time, when a person wanted to send a letter to another country, he or she (if they were feeling generous) could also send the recipient an international reply coupon. The coupon could then be used to pay for the postage of the reply. Ponzi's idea was to buy cheap reply coupons in another country and sell them in the United States, where they were worth more. He then planned to share the profits with his investors. However, transporting and paying for the coupons caused delays and incurred extra costs, which meant he couldn't pay back his investors as quickly as he had promised. But he didn't tell them that. [1]____ Ponzi paid the early investors their profit with the new money that was pouring in, and kept some of it for himself. At the height of his success, he was buying and selling around 160 million reply coupons, despite only 27,000 existing worldwide. When people realized this, it was all over. [2]____

How does it work?

The Ponzi scheme is based on a simple principle revolving around paying old investors with money that comes in from new investors. What exactly they invest in doesn't matter. With the money from the first investors you rent a fancy office and buy a new car, which helps you to attract new investors. [3]____. One person can only do so much, and sooner or later the scheme flops because there aren't enough new investors to pay all of the old ones.

Other big schemers

Examples of the Ponzi scheme date back as far as the 1880s, and are still happening now. One of the longest-running operations was headed by Lou Pearlman, former manager of the famous American boy bands Backstreet Boys and N*Sync. To fund promotional activity for his band roster, he convinced businesspeople to invest in other nonexistent side projects. [4]____ Pearlman was eventually convicted of cheating investors of over $300 million and, in 2008, was sentenced to 25 years imprisonment.

But that was nothing compared to Bernard Madoff's $65 billion Ponzi scheme. In 2009 Madoff was sentenced to 150 years in prison after having cheated billionaires, celebrities, and even banks and charities. [5]____ He was also helped by the fact that he was running a legitimate business at the same time. He didn't promise ridiculously high returns, and he always gave his investors their money when they asked for it. Madoff's business propositions seemed perfectly trustworthy, but a lot of people lost all their money.

So for Charles Ponzi, Lou Pearlman, Bernard Madoff, and countless other Ponzi schemers, their lies eventually caught up with them. Their riches were only temporary and the price they eventually had to pay was much more. Our advice? Never try to make an honest buck based on a lie. The truth always wins... eventually.

CHARLES PONZI

2 VOCABULARY business

a Complete the text with the correct form of a verb from the box.

become	expand	export	import
launch	market	~~set up~~	take over

A friend of mine, Anne, was lucky enough to inherit a farm when she graduated from college, so she decided to [1] _set up_ her own organic food business. The company [2] _____ its products under the name of Bioplus and one of the most successful products it makes is granola. Not all of the ingredients come from the farm. Anne [3] _____ the nuts and dried fruit from South America. She mixes these with her own cereal products to make the granola. Regionally, her granola sells well, but she also [4] _____ to East Coast states like New York and New Jersey.

The company is [5] _____ rapidly and Anne is always looking for new employees. Right now she's preparing to [6] _____ a new cereal bar the company has been testing. Anne is very realistic because she knows she will never [7] _____ the market leader in the field, but neither does she want one of the big cereal giants like Kelloggs or Nestlé to [8] _____ her company.

b Complete the sentences with the correct form of *make* or *do*.

1 A company always _does_ extensive market research before it launches a new product.
2 If a company _____ a loss, the staff members often face job cuts.
3 Many countries started _____ business with China when the trade sanctions were lifted.
4 The managing director _____ the decision to close the factory yesterday.
5 The company president _____ a deal with management to increase overtime pay yesterday.
6 The factory was _____ badly, so in the end it closed down.
7 Companies always _____ market research before they launch a new product.
8 If we _____ a profit again next year, the manager may think of opening another office.

c Complete the crossword.

Clues across →

3 The average McDonald's restaurant serves 1,584…per day.
4 TGI Friday's is an American restaurant…with over 920 restaurants.
6 The law firm of Clifford Chance gives legal advice to…in 25 countries.
7 The…of SpaceX is in Los Angeles, California.

Clues down ↓

1 Google Inc. is a…company that operates all over the world.
2 There is a…of Bank of America on many main streets in the US.
4 Steve Jobs was the…of Apple Inc. from 2000 to 2011.
5 Amancio Ortega is the…of the Spanish clothing chain Zara.

3 MINI GRAMMAR *whatever, whenever, etc.*

Complete the dialogues using *whatever, whichever, whoever, whenever, however,* or *wherever.*

1 **A** Where would you like to go for dinner tonight?
  B _Wherever_ you want. I don't mind.
2 **A** Do you want tea or coffee?
  B I don't mind. _____ is easiest.
3 **A** What should I buy you for your birthday?
  B I don't mind. I'll be happy with _____ you give me.
4 **A** How often does your boyfriend go to the gym?
  B He goes _____ he can.
5 **A** Can I bring my new boyfriend to your party?
  B Sure. Bring _____ you want.
6 **A** I'm not sure how we should decorate the living room.
  B Decorate it _____ you want. You have great taste.

4 GRAMMAR clauses of contrast and purpose

a (Circle) the correct answer.

1 *Although* / *Despite* she's the head of the department, she often goes out with her colleagues.

2 The account manager called his client *for* / *to* arrange a meeting.

3 The company is expanding *even though* / *in spite of* there is a recession.

4 The firm closed several of its smaller office buildings *in order to* / *so that* cut costs.

5 His secretary stayed at her desk *to not* / *so as not to* miss an important phone call.

6 Everybody seemed to enjoy Mike's speech at the wedding *in spite of* / *even though* his terrible jokes.

7 The restaurant staff members are happy *despite* / *although* working long hours every day.

8 She closed the door to her office *so as to* / *so that* nobody could hear her conversation.

b Complete the second sentence so that it has a similar meaning to the first sentence using the word or phrase in bold.

1 Although he's the managing director, he goes to work by bike.
despite
He goes to work by bike *despite being the managing director* .

2 Although they don't do any marketing, their products sell well.
in spite of
Their products sell well _____.

3 They reduced their prices so as to sell more products. **so that**
They reduced their prices _____.

4 I have to leave work by six o' clock so that I don't miss my train.
so as not to
I have to leave work by six o' clock _____.

5 Despite the fact that I was late, my boss wasn't angry. **although**
My boss wasn't angry _____.

5 PRONUNCIATION

changing stress on nouns and verbs

a [ONLINE] Listen and complete the sentences.

1 China *exports* more goods than any other country.

2 Vinyl _____ are becoming popular again.

3 There's been a huge _____ in gas prices recently.

4 You can only lose weight if you _____ the amount of calories you eat.

5 Scientists are making _____ on finding a cure for AIDS.

6 The visa _____ you to stay for three months.

7 Brazil _____ about a third of the world's coffee.

8 We do not give _____ without a valid receipt.

b Underline the stressed syllable on the words you wrote in **a**.

c Listen and check. Then listen and repeat the sentences.

6 LISTENING

a [ONLINE] Listen to a radio phone-in program about Mr. Americo Lopes who bought a winning lottery ticket, but didn't share it with his coworkers. How many of the callers think that he did the right thing?

b Listen again and mark the sentences **T** (true) or **F** (false).

1 Mr. Lopes bought the lottery ticket in December of 2009. ____

2 Mr. Lopes was a factory worker. ____

3 The jury decided Mr. Lopes must share his prize money with his coworkers. ____

4 Caller 1 believes Mr. Lopes should share information about his life with his friends and coworkers. ____

5 Caller 2 says people make questionable decisions when a lot of money is involved. ____

6 Caller 3 thinks the jury made the correct decision. ____

7 Caller 4 says the man had a moral obligation to share the ticket winnings. ____

8 Caller 5 feels some anger toward the man. ____

c Listen again with the audio script on p.75 and try to guess the meaning of any words that you don't know. Then check in your dictionary.

USEFUL WORDS AND PHRASES

Learn these words and phrases.

ad/ advertisement /æd/ædvər'taɪzmənt/

advertising campaign /'ædvərtaɪzɪŋ kæm'peɪn/

airbrush (a photo) /'ɛrbrʌʃ/

appeal /ə'pil/

brand /brænd/

claim (v and noun) /kleɪm/

commercial /kə'mərʃl/

consumers /kən'sumərz/

jingle /'dʒɪŋgl/

misleading (statements) /mɪs'lidɪŋ/

slogan /'slovgən/

sue (somebody) /su/

A city is a large community where people are lonely together.

Herbert Prochnow, US banking executive

9B Megacities

1 READING

a Read the article quickly and choose the word that best describes Shanghai, according to the writer.

a dangerous b stimulating c modern d polluted

b Read the article again and choose the correct answers.

1 Puxi and Pudong are…
   a two cities near Shanghai.
   b two districts of Shanghai.
   c two rivers crossing Shanghai.
   d two people from Shanghai.

2 The residents of Shanghai often go outside because…
   a they don't have enough space at home.
   b the weather is always fine.
   c the food stalls sell good food.
   d they need fresh air to do their hobbies.

3 The roads of Shanghai are dangerous because…
   a there are no traffic lights.
   b drivers do not obey the rules.
   c there is too much traffic.
   d pedestrians do not use the crossings.

4 Tourists visiting Shanghai should always…
   a use public transportation.
   b travel with a guide.
   c avoid talking to strangers.
   d be careful when they arrive.

5 According to the writer, Shanghai is special because it has…
   a a lot of historical monuments.
   b an excellent public transportation system.
   c a mixture of different things to see and do.
   d the best hotels in the country.

c Look at the highlighted words and phrases in the text. What do you think they mean? Use your dictionary to look up their meaning and pronunciation.

Shanghai, with a population of around 23.5 million, is currently the fifth of the world's megacities. Its location on the mouth of the Yangtze River Delta in eastern China makes it one of the busiest ports in the world. The Huang Pu River, a tributary of the Yangtze, separates the historic center of the city, the Puxi area, from the newly developed financial and commercial area called Pudong.

On their arrival in Shanghai, visitors are hit by an explosion of sights, sounds, and smells. Rents are high, and apartments tiny, so most residents prefer to hang out outside. The street is a place to eat, play, read, and relax, and it is not unusual to see people strolling around in their nightgowns and pajamas. The street serves as an extension of the workplace as well. Hair stylists sit their customers on chairs outside their salons to cut their hair, and there are food stalls on every street corner piled high with delicious steamed buns filled with meat, vegetables, or mushrooms.

However, it is not only the sidewalk that is crowded. Despite the extensive metro system – Shanghai has the third longest network in the world – the traffic in the city is terrible. During rush hour, it can take two hours to drive a 30-minute route. In general, drivers do not like to follow the rules of the road, and they regularly ignore speed limits and traffic lights. This makes crossing the road extremely hazardous for pedestrians, whose safety is not guaranteed even when the green light is showing. In China, road accidents are the major cause of death for people between the ages of 15 and 45, with an estimated 600 traffic deaths per day.

But as far as crime is concerned, Shanghai is a relatively safe city. You rarely hear of crimes being committed, although pickpockets are known to operate in crowded areas and tourists are sometimes the target for scams. The most common of these consist of unofficial taxi drivers overcharging passengers for the ride to their hotel from the airport, or bar owners getting an accomplice to bring an unsuspecting tourist to their bar only to present him with a terribly high check when he tries to leave. In general, however, the Chinese are very friendly to foreigners and they treat them with a lot of respect. Nonnative residents usually become good friends with their Chinese neighbors, once they have gotten used to each other.

The city of Shanghai offers a fusion of East and West; old and new. Visitors staying at the brand new five-star Ritz Carlton Hotel can explore the ancient Buddhist temples when they go sightseeing. Passengers travel on the Shanghai Meglev, the fastest train in the world, while messengers transport impossible loads on their bicycles. Sometimes, the contrasts can be exhausting, but one thing is certain: Shanghai is a city where nobody ever feels bored.

2 VOCABULARY prefixes and suffixes

a Complete the sentences with the prefixes from the box.

~~anti~~ auto bi mega mis mono
multi over post sub under

1 The doctor prescribed _anti_biotics for my brother's chest infection.
2 There was a food shortage in many countries during the _____war period, between 1946 and 1960.
3 Some of the residents of megacities live in _____standard housing.
4 My English teacher recommends us to use a _____lingual dictionary, one that is only in English.
5 My colleagues are always complaining that they are _____worked and _____paid.
6 The leader of the protest used a _____phone to make himself heard.
7 You couldn't miss Sandra – she was the one in the _____colored coat.
8 The town has just celebrated its _____centennial.
9 Hundreds of fans were waiting for the singer hoping to get an _____graph.
10 It's a popular _____conception that cold weather can make you sick. This is simply not true.

b Complete the sentences with nouns formed from the words in parentheses.

1 I borrowed the money with the _intention_ of giving it back to you. (intend)
2 His greatest _____ is his inability to express his feelings. (weak)
3 There is a general _____ that house prices will rise before the end of the year. (believe)
4 You need to have _____ and stamina to become a professional athlete. (strong)
5 He wasn't chosen for the basketball team because of his _____. (high)
6 Teachers are trying to fight _____ in schools throughout the country. (race)
7 The _____ of online shopping means that fewer people are shopping in the malls. (convenient)
8 Gandhi was a humanist who believed in the _____ of man. (brother)
9 There's been a great _____ in public transportation recently. (improve)
10 I didn't have much _____ finding work in the city, so I moved back to the country. (succeed)

3 GRAMMAR uncountable and plural nouns

a Circle the correct answer. Check (✓) if both are possible.

1 Can I have *a piece of bread | some bread*, please? ✓
2 My grandmother suffers from (*bad health*)| *a bad health*.
3 I bought *a new piece of furniture | some new furniture* for my living room.
4 Can you please give me *a piece of advice | some advice*?
5 We lost *a luggage | a piece of luggage* on the way back from Singapore.
6 Jackie's upset because she's had *a bad news | some bad news*.
7 Be careful with that vase – it's made of *glass | a glass*.
8 My girlfriend gave me *a pair of pajamas | some pajamas* for my birthday.
9 The teacher gave the boy extra points for *a good behavior | good behavior*.
10 Can you lend me *a paper | some paper*? I left my notebook at home.

b Complete the sentences with *is* or *are*.

1 My clothes _are_ really wet. I got caught in a thunderstorm.
2 The traffic _____ terrible during rush hour in the city.
3 John's climbing equipment _____ very heavy. I can hardly pick it up.
4 The new research into sleep patterns _____ fascinating.
5 The outskirts of the town _____ run-down and a little bit depressing.
6 The good news _____ that we're getting married in the spring!
7 The flight crew on this plane _____ very young.
8 Politics _____ really fascinating – particularly for politicians!
9 Do you think my belongings _____ safe in the hotel room?
10 Police _____ investigating the murder of an elderly woman in her home.

4 PRONUNCIATION

word stress with prefixes and suffixes

a <u>Underline</u> the main (primary) stress in the words in the box. Then write them in the correct place in the chart.

an|ti|so|cial   bi|lin|gual   con|ven|ience   en|ter|tain|ment
ex|cite|ment   friend|li|ness   go|vern|ment   ig|no|rance
o|ver|crow|ded   po|ver|ty   re|duc|tion   un|em|ploy|ment

Stress on 1st syllable	Stress on 2nd syllable	Stress on 3rd syllable
_____	_____	*antisocial*
_____	_____	_____
_____	_____	_____
_____	_____	_____

b **ONLINE** Listen and check. Then listen and repeat the words.

5 LISTENING

a **ONLINE** Listen to five people talking about their favorite big cities. Match five of the cities in the box to the speakers.

Auckland   Boston   Buenos Aires   Hong Kong   Melbourne
Montreal   Rio de Janeiro   Seoul   Vancouver   Washington, D.C.

Speaker 1 _____   Speaker 4 _____

Speaker 2 _____   Speaker 5 _____

Speaker 3 _____

b Listen again and match the speakers with the sentences. There is one sentence which you do not need to use.

Speaker number
↓

☐ **A** You can go sightseeing here, but you can also relax by the ocean.

☐ **B** It's the perfect place to go if you want to see a particular dance.

☐ **C** The city is surrounded by areas of stunning natural beauty.

☐ **D** It has a reputation for having the best nightlife in the world.

☐ **E** It's a city where two different ways of life exist side by side.

☐ **F** It's a great place to visit if you're interested in history.

c Listen again with the audio script on p.76 and try to guess the meaning of any words that you don't know. Then check in your dictionary.

USEFUL WORDS AND PHRASES

Learn these words and phrases.

alienation /ˌeɪliəˈneɪʃn/
automated subway /ˈɔtəˌmeɪtɪd ˈsʌbweɪ/
commuters /kəˈmyutərz/
inhabitants /ɪnˈhæbətənts/
loneliness /ˈloʊnlinəs/
population /pɑpyəˈleɪʃn/
poverty /ˈpɑvərti/
traffic fumes /ˈtræfɪk fyumz/
unthinkable /ʌnˈθɪŋkəbl/
wealthy /ˈwɛlθi/

ONLINE FILE 9

1 LOOKING AT LANGUAGE

Complete the sentences with a phrase from the box.

an earworm	a captive audience	get into your head
had their day	hit a false note	their ears perk up
word for word		

1 The best way to get rid of _an earworm_ is to replace it with another tune.

2 Some people say that libraries have _____ and they will soon disappear.

3 The song has a catchy chorus that can easily _____ and you find yourself singing it all day.

4 I repeated her instructions _____ to avoid any confusion.

5 My dogs love dog biscuits – _____ as soon as they hear me open the package.

6 Musicians often play in train stations and ask for money because they know they have _____.

7 The politician _____ with her speech and caused a lot of controversy.

2 READING

a Read the article and match headings A–D to paragraphs 1–4.

A **Leaving it Late**   C **One-Man Show**
B **Gender Gap**   D **All Play, No Work**

b Read the article. Mark the sentences **T** (true) or **F** (false).

1 *Mad Men* is a comedy drama series. ____

2 Don Draper is portrayed as a hero in the series. ____

3 A modern advertising campaign involves many people working together. ____

4 A lot of planning goes into Don Draper's pitches. ____

5 The executives at Sterling, Cooper, Draper, Pryce work extremely hard. ____

6 In a real ad agency there is never time to relax. ____

7 Most of the women at Sterling, Cooper, Draper, Pryce are secretaries. ____

8 A large proportion of creative directors in advertising agencies today are women. ____

c Look at the highlighted words and phrases. What do you think they mean? Use your dictionary to look up their meaning and pronunciation.

Mad Men:
fact or fiction in the world of advertising today?

Many people have been introduced to the world of advertising through the American drama series *Mad Men*, which follows the lives of people working for an important advertising agency on Madison Avenue in New York in the 1960s (hence the name Mad Men). However, the advertising industry has progressed and developed in many ways since then. Here are some examples of how things are different today.

1 ____
Sterling, Cooper, Draper, Pryce is the fictional name of *Mad Men*'s advertising agency and the action revolves around its creative director, Don Draper. All of the agency's work is heavily dependent upon Draper's creative talent and he is constantly called upon to save the day. However, his ability to instantly solve advertising problems single-handedly does not reflect what happens these days. In fact, advertising agencies are made up of different teams that work together and most projects are part of one massive and coordinated campaign. The fate of a real-life campaign rarely lies in the hands of one individual.

2 ____
Mad Men is well-known for its improvised "pitches" (presentations to potential clients) that seem to come out of nowhere. Often it is Don Draper himself who suddenly manages to effortlessly transform a vague idea he has had into advertising gold. This portrayal gives the impression that the most successful approach for pitching a new idea to a potential client is to put off the work for as long as possible. This could not be further from the truth, however, and in real life it takes a lot of hard work and creative genius to make a successful pitch.

3 ____
The atmosphere at Sterling, Cooper, Draper, Pryce is one where anything goes. From long lunches to midday naps in the office, it seems as if there is never anything to be done. In the real world, an agency's workload can vary from one extreme to another depending on the client's demands and the corresponding deadlines. One week, the team may have more time to play while the next they have no time to sleep. This is the nature of the job and a great deal of work goes into every single project, even though there are times when the employees are able to take a break.

4 ____
In *Mad Men*, the female characters have been carefully researched so that they coincide with the views of American society at the time. In the 1960s, few women went on to further their education, and those who did often became secretaries or nurses. This situation is reflected at the agency, where sexism is rife and all but one of the executives is male. The exception, Peggy Olson, is regarded as an oddball by her colleagues. Fortunately, the situation these days has greatly improved regarding sexism in the workplace. However, still only a tiny percentage of today's creative directors are women.

Mad Men is one of the most popular period drama series ever shown on American television. It has been widely praised for its historical authenticity, visual style, costume design, acting, writing, and directing and it has won many awards.

In science the credit goes to the man who convinces the world, not to the man to whom the idea first occurs.

Francis Darwin, botanist and son of Charles Darwin

10A The dark side of the moon

1 GRAMMAR quantifiers: *all*, *every*, etc.

a Right (✓) or wrong (✗)? Correct the mistakes in the highlighted phrases.

1 I've taken all luggage up to our room, OK? ✗ *all the luggage*
2 Everybody were bad-tempered because it was late. _____
3 All went wrong at my last job interview. _____
4 On Wednesday I spent all day studying for my biology exam. _____
5 All the men love buying new electronic gadgets. _____
6 We go bike riding on the rail trail every morning during the week. _____
7 The most people are against eating genetically modified food. _____
8 Every classroom in that school has an interactive whiteboard. _____

b Complete the dialogues with *no*, *any*, or *none*.

1 **A** Can I have a cookie?
  B Sorry, we don't have _any_.
2 **A** How much homework have you done?
  B _____. I don't feel like it right now.
3 **A** How are we going to get home?
  B By taxi. There aren't _____ buses at this time of night.
4 **A** Did any of your friends pass the exam?
  B No, _____ of them. It was too difficult.
5 **A** Let's have dinner in our hotel room.
  B We can't. There's _____ room service after 9 p.m.
6 **A** When can you come?
  B _____ day you like. I'm free all week.

c Complete the sentences with a word from the box.

both   either   neither   nor

1 _Both_ my brother and my sister have children.
2 Dave has two computers, but _____ of them is working.
3 We'd like to go to _____ Cancun or Acapulco for our vacation this year.
4 Neither my boyfriend _____ I eat meat.
5 _____ of their children are at the same college.
6 I can't decide between these two shirts. I like _____ of them.
7 _____ of my parents have ever been overseas.

2 VOCABULARY science

a Complete the sentences with a word from the same family as the words in **bold**.

1 I always knew, right from the start, that I wanted to be a _scientist_. **science**
2 Factories manufacturing plastics produce a lot of _____ waste. **chemistry**
3 My daughter's best subject at school is _____. **biologist**
4 One of the most controversial issues of our time is _____ engineering. **gene**
5 _____ is a mystery to me. I failed every exam I ever took. **physicist**

b Match each verb to a suitable noun.

1 be   a a discovery
2 carry out   b a theory
3 make   c a guinea pig
4 prove   d new drugs
5 test   e an experiment

c Complete the sentences with the correct form of a verb phrase from **b**.

1 We _carried out an experiment_ in our chemistry class, but it went terribly wrong!
2 The student volunteered to _____ _____ because he needed the money.
3 Researchers _____ an important _____ completely by accident last month.
4 Companies need to _____ to make sure they are safe.
5 It took a long time for Newton to _____ his _____ of gravity.

63

3 READING

a Look at the pictures and read the article. Match each picture to a paragraph.

b Read the article again and answer the questions. Write the letter of the paragraph.

Which inventor…

1 thought of something that made an extra tool unnecessary? ____

2 made it safer to carry something? ____

3 found the answer to a security problem? ____

4 came from outside the country where he created his invention? ____

5 invented something that was an improvement on the existing design? ____

6 was British? ____

7 invented something that speeded up the manufacturing process? ____

8 had to take legal action against a colleague? ____

9 designed something that can be fitted onto something else? ____

10 had an idea outside work? ____

Unknown inventors

For most of us, the word "inventor" makes us think of names like Alexander Graham Bell or Guglielmo Marconi, the men behind the telephone and the radio. But what about the people whose inventions we use so often that we forget someone had to think them up in the first place? Read on to find out about five of the unknown inventors of our times.

A An American woman named Margaret Knight was working in a paper bag factory when she noticed how difficult it was to put things into the bags. So, she decided to invent a machine that folded and glued paper to make a flat-bottomed bag. She made a lot of sketches of her machine, but before she could actually make it, another employee named Charles Annan stole her idea. Knight took Annan to court and eventually won the case. In 1858, Knight set up her own paper bag company and received large sums of royalties for her invention when other companies made her bags under license.

B In 1910, a Russian-born candy manufacturer named Sam Born emigrated to the US and set up a business there. One day, when he was wondering how to make the candy-making process more efficient, he thought up an idea for a new machine. It was called the Born Sucker Machine and its job was to quickly and mechanically insert the sticks into lollipops. The new machine helped make the candy and Sam's company into a huge success, and in 1916, he was awarded "the key to San Francisco." In 1923, he founded the Just Born company, which is still going strong in the US today.

C In 1959, Ernie Fraze, the owner of a successful American engineering company, was at a picnic when he went to fetch the drinks. In those days, drinks were in sealed cans that were opened with a can opener. Unfortunately, Ernie had forgotten to bring the opener. This started him thinking, and one night, when he was having trouble sleeping, he solved the can dilemma. His idea was a new can that could be easily opened with a ring pull. Ernie's company began manufacturing a system of mass producing these cans and by 1980, he was making over $500 million dollars a year from his invention.

D Once the banks had decided they wanted to install ATMs, the next problem was how to confirm a customer's identity to allow money to be withdrawn. It was a Scottish man by the name of James Goodfellow who came up with the solution. In 1966, Goodfellow realized he could link a set of numbers, known only to the account owner, to an encoded card. If the two numbers matched, the person would receive their cash. This number became known as a Personal Identification Number or PIN. Goodfellow didn't get a penny for his idea, but he did receive an award from the Queen of England.

E When take-out cups of coffee became popular, the Solo Cup Company, a leading producer of disposable cups, saw a hole in the market for a new container. Jack Clements was the man they asked to design it. In 1985, Clements designed a new lid for the cup in the shape of a dome. The lid rested comfortably between the mouth and nose when the user took a sip and it also helped prevent spilling. Since then, the Solo Traveler Lid has been adopted by many of America's coffeehouses and it has helped Clements' company earn $2 billion of annual income.

c Look at the highlighted words and phrases in the text and try to figure out their meaning. Then use them to complete the sentences.

1 After brainstorming solutions to the problem, researchers _____ a new idea.

2 When companies see _____, there is a lot of competition to fill it.

3 I couldn't get any more cash out of the ATM because I had already _____ $250.

4 The designers made a lot of _____ before they decided on the final version.

5 You shouldn't put a drink on your desk because you run the risk of _____ it on your computer.

6 They have started _____ the gadgets to meet the increased demand.

7 My grandfather is _____ although he is 94 years old.

8 Musicians earn _____ every time their song is played on the radio.

4 PRONUNCIATION changing stress

a Look at the words. Is the stress on the same syllable? Check (✓) the correct column. Use your dictionary to help you.

	same syllable	different syllable
1 bi|o|lo|gy / bi|o|lo|gi|cal	____	✓
2 che|mist / che|mi|stry	____	____
3 dis|co|ver / dis|co|ve|ry	____	____
4 ex|per|i|ment / ex|per|i|men|tal	____	____
5 ge|ne|tic / ge|ne|ti|cist	____	____
6 phy|sics / phy|si|cist	____	____
7 sci|en|tist / sci|en|ti|fic	____	____
8 theor|y / theor|e|ti|cal	____	____

b ONLINE Listen and check. Mark the stressed syllables. Then listen and repeat the words.

5 LISTENING

a ONLINE Listen to the radio program about NASA inventions and number the pictures in the order they are mentioned.

b Listen again and complete the sentences with between one and three words.

1 The first smoke detectors were invented in order to detect a fire or if there were _____ on the US space station *Skylab*.

2 NASA's smoke detector had a new feature that allowed astronauts to adjust the _____ to prevent false alarms.

3 The disadvantage of plastic glasses is that they _____ easily.

4 NASA developed a _____ to protect astronauts' helmets.

5 NASA uses infrared technology to _____ of stars.

6 Diatek wanted to _____ of time that it took for nurses to take patients' temperatures.

c Listen again with the audio script on p.76 and try to guess the meaning of any words that you don't know. Then check in your dictionary.

USEFUL WORDS AND PHRASES

Learn these words and phrases.

anesthetic /ˌænəsˈθɛtɪk/
blood transfusion /ˈblʌd trænsˈfyuʒn/
blood donor /blʌd doʊnər/
inhale (a gas) /ɪnˈheɪl/
lead (poisoning) /lɛd/
lethal dose /ˈliθl doʊs/
nuclear bomb /ˈnukliər bɑm/
radiation /reɪdiˈeɪʃn/

There are always three speeches, for every one you actually gave. The one you practiced, the one you gave, and the one you wish you had given.

Dale Carnegie, American lecturer

10B The power of words

1 READING

a Read the article once. Why didn't Marlon Brando accept his Oscar?

b Read the article again and choose the correct answer.

1 For the writer, the most interesting part of the Oscars ceremony is when…
  a we find out who has won each category.
  b the celebrities pose for photographs.
  c the winners speak.
  d we see excerpts from the nominated movies.

2 When Sacheen Littlefeather went up on stage, she…
  a refused to accept the Oscar statuette.
  b greeted the two presenters.
  c announced the winning actor.
  d turned off the microphone.

3 Marlon Brando was protesting because he thought that the movie industry should…
  a employ more Native Americans in their movies.
  b apologize to Native Americans.
  c return the Pine Ridge reservation to Native Americans.
  d stop contributing to a negative stereotype of Native Americans.

4 While Ms. Littlefeather was speaking, the people in the audience…
  a sat in silence.
  b were divided in their opinion.
  c showed their support.
  d wanted her to stop.

5 After Marlon Brando's boycott, the organizers of the ceremony…
  a declared their support for Native Americans.
  b reduced the length of acceptance speeches.
  c changed the rules for who could pick up Oscars.
  d gave an award to Sacheen Littlefeather.

c Look at the highlighted words and phrases in the text. What do you think they mean? Use your dictionary to look up their meaning and pronunciation.

CONFUSION AND CONTROVERSY AT THE OSCARS

Every year, movie-goers all over the world eagerly await the annual Academy Awards ceremony, better known as the Oscars. The red carpet is rolled out, the actors are photographed in their elegant gowns and tuxedos, and the winners are announced. And then comes the moment of truth: the acceptance speeches. Some of these are more memorable than others, but none will be remembered more than one that was made at the 45th Academy Awards ceremony of 1973. This is what happened.

The moment had arrived for the announcement of the winner of the Oscar for Best Actor. The award was to be presented by Roger Moore, who was the current James Bond, and Norwegian actress Liv Ullman. The two opened the envelope and announced the name of the winner: Marlon Brando for his role as Vito Corleone in the movie *The Godfather*. To everyone's surprise, it was not Mr. Brando who came on stage, but a young woman in Native American dress. The woman was a Native American activist named Sacheen Littlefeather. She proceeded to brush aside Roger Moore when he tried to give her the statuette and made her way toward the microphone. Here she gave a 60-second speech introducing herself, explaining why she was there instead of the famous actor, and apologizing for interrupting the ceremony. The audience – and the presenters – were shocked!

The reason for Mr. Brando's absence was that he was boycotting the ceremony. In previous years, he had become increasingly upset by the treatment of American Indians on television and in movies, where they were always portrayed as savage and evil. He was also very concerned about an ongoing incident on the Pine Ridge Reservation in South Dakota. Tired of their corrupt leader, who was backed by the US government, a group of armed Native Americans had taken over the town of Wounded Knee. At the time of the Oscar ceremony, the Native Americans were still holding the town against US officials, including the FBI.

Mr. Brando had written down the reasons for his boycott in a 15-page speech that he had given Ms. Littlefeather to read at the ceremony. The organizers, however, had prohibited her from making this speech, so she had gone ahead and improvised with her own much shorter version, which caused quite a stir. Halfway through, some of the audience started booing and others began to cheer. Yet she continued bravely to the end and then allowed the two presenters to escort her backstage, where she shared Mr. Brando's original speech with the press. The next day it was printed in its entirety in the *New York Times*.

Ms. Littlefeather received several death threats after her intervention at the Oscar ceremony, but she continued fighting for the cause and still works with the Native American community today. The Wounded Knee incident finished after 73 days and succeeded in making Americans more aware of the injustice suffered by American Indians in their country. And as far as the Oscar ceremony is concerned, it was the last time that an actor was allowed to nominate someone else to accept an award on his or her behalf.

2 GRAMMAR articles

a Complete the sayings with *a*, *an*, *the*, or no article (—).

1 All you need is ___ love.
2 He's _____ man of his word.
3 ____ women are from Venus; ____ men are from Mars.
4 _____ time waits for no man.
5 Don't worry! It's not ____ end of ____ world!
6 That's ____ life!
7 It's ____ small world.
8 ____ actions speak louder than ____ words.

b Complete the sentences with *the* where necessary.

1 The toy industry in ___ China is the biggest in the world.

2 There are 50 states in ___ US.

3 ___ 5 Freeway was closed yesterday because of the floods.

4 ___ Central Park is one of ___ largest green spaces in New York City.

5 Edmund Hillary was ___ first man to climb ___ Mount Everest.

6 ___ Lake Victoria is ___ largest lake in ___ Africa.

7 ___ Panama Canal connects the Atlantic Ocean to ___ Pacific Ocean.

8 ___ Balearic Islands are situated in ___ Mediterranean Sea.

c Right (✓) or wrong (✗)? Correct the mistakes in the highlighted phrases.

1 The college in my town has a very good reputation. ✓ _____
2 Mae-Ting can't still be at the work. It's really late. ✗ *at work* _____
3 The man has gone to the prison for the crimes he committed when he was younger. _____
4 Daisy takes advantage of the time her children are at the school to take an online course. _____
5 The prison is on the outskirts of the city. _____
6 Somebody broke into my parents' house while they were at the church. _____
7 Did you have time to finish the work I left for you? _____
8 My boyfriend's in the college. He's studying architecture. _____
9 My brother teaches at the elementary school that we both attended. _____
10 The church in my village dates back to the fifteenth century. _____

3 VOCABULARY collocation: word pairs

a Find the word pairs in the box and link them with *and* or *or*. Then complete the sentences.

all bed breakfast fork ~~jelly~~ knife later less
more never nothing now once peace
~~peanut butter~~ pepper quiet salt sooner twice

1 Would you like a _peanut butter and jelly_ sandwich for lunch today?
2 I enjoy the _____ of the countryside when we go for a walk.
3 I got a new wisdom tooth. I suppose I'll have to go to the dentist _____.
4 It takes a long time for children to learn how to eat with a _____ well.
5 We stayed in a cheap _____ when we visited Toronto.
6 Nathan has _____ finished his homework – all he has to do now is to print it out.
7 It's _____ with Sue; either she calls every day or you don't hear from her for weeks.
8 This soup doesn't have any taste. Can you pass the _____, please?
9 Patricia's about to leave, so it's _____ – I may not get another chance to ask her out.
10 I've been skiing _____, but I'm not very good at it.

b Complete the word pair idioms.

1 There wasn't much left at the furniture sale, just a few o*dds* and e_____.
2 I'm s_____ and t_____ of having to clean up after my children.
3 She left her husband because there wasn't any g_____ and t_____ in their marriage.
4 My life has its u_____ and d_____, but in general I'm very happy.
5 The streets were very dangerous because of the lack of l_____ and o_____ in the city.
6 We arrived s_____ and s_____ after a three-day journey through the mountains.
7 I have no idea what we're having for lunch because my wife told me to w_____ and s_____.
8 We go to the movies n_____ and a_____, but more often than not we just watch a movie on TV.

4 PRONUNCIATION /ðə/ or /ði/

a Check (✓) the correct pronunciation of *the*.

	/ðə/	/ði/
1 I left my coat in the backseat of my car.	✓	___
2 The accident happened last night.	___	___
3 The clocks fall back next weekend.	___	___
4 The uniform my sister wears to school is awful.	___	___
5 Have you ever been to the US?	___	___
6 The end of that movie was really sad.	___	___

b ONLINE Listen and check. Then listen and repeat the sentences.

USEFUL WORDS AND PHRASES

Learn these words and phrases.

apartheid /əˈpɑrteɪt/
battle /ˈbætl/
go on (to the end) /goʊ ɑn/
hunger strike /ˈhʌŋgər straɪk/
invasion /ɪnˈveɪʒn/
make a speech /meɪk ə spitʃ/
quote /kwoʊt/
sacred /ˈseɪkrəd/
sacrifice /ˈsækrəfaɪs/
surrender /səˈrɛndər/

---

5 LISTENING

a ONLINE Listen to a radio program about an English king with a stammer. Choose the correct answer.

1 The king with the stammer was…
   a George V.
   b Edward VIII.
   c George VI.
2 The man who helped him overcome his stammer was…
   a his wife's therapist.
   b an actor.
   c his father's doctor.
3 The King had to give his most important speech…
   a at the end of the British Empire Exhibition.
   b when his brother abdicated as King.
   c at the beginning of an international conflict.

b Listen again and answer the questions.

1 What was the King's name when he was a child?
2 What did his father make him do?
3 Who was unkind to him when he was little?
4 In which year did he make his first disastrous speech?
5 How did his father's doctors try to treat him?
6 Where did his new therapist treat him?
7 How long was it before the treatment showed results?
8 Why did his brother abdicate?
9 Who was with the King when he made his important speech?
10 What did the therapist say after the speech that was unusual?

c Listen again with the audio script on p.77 and try to guess the meaning of any words that you don't know. Then check in your dictionary.

ONLINE FILE 10

Listening

1 A))

Interviewer Hello, Mr. Bridges?

Applicant Yes, hello. I'm Stephen Bridges.

Interviewer Good morning. My name's Jenny Howarth.

Applicant Nice to meet you, Ms. Howarth.

Interviewer Would you like to get some coffee before we start?

Applicant Oh, no thank you.

Interviewer All right, please come in and take a seat.

Applicant Thank you.

Interviewer You had no trouble finding us this morning, then?

Applicant Yes, it was easy. I took the subway to 42nd Street, and then I walked. It's a beautiful morning.

Interviewer Yes, it is. So you're here for the position of hotel receptionist, is that right?

Applicant Yes, that's right. I saw your ad on the Complete Jobs website and I decided to apply.

Interviewer You know that this is only a temporary position, don't you Mr. Bridges?

Applicant Yes, I do. And that's ideal for me. I'm moving across the country in three months, so it fits in perfectly with my plans.

Interviewer Really? Where are you going to go?

Applicant Well, I just graduated from college with a degree in Modern Languages, and I'm going to graduate school to work on a Master's degree in California in September to study applied linguistics. My cousin lives there so I'm going to stay with him, which I'm really looking forward to. We get along really well and he knows all the best restaurants to visit. He's been living in California for a couple of years now, and I've been to see him a few times …

Interviewer Yes, well, back to you, Mr. Bridges, have you had any experience working in a hotel reception?

Applicant Yes, I have. Last summer, I spent a month at Fiesta Hotel in Playa del Carmen. My Spanish improved a lot while I was there, and I also learned a lot about customer care. Some of my colleagues were a little bit difficult sometimes, but in general, we worked well as a team.

Interviewer I see. You mentioned Spanish, Mr. Bridges. Which other languages do you speak?

Applicant I speak Spanish, French, and a little Italian. From my research, I believe most of your guests are from South America, is that right?

Interviewer Yes, but we also have some customers from Asia, mainly Japan. Do you think this would cause you any difficulties?

Applicant Not at all, I'm a good communicator, so we would be able to understand each other.

Interviewer Tell me how you would deal with a difficult guest, for example someone who thinks there is a mistake with the bill.

Applicant I don't think I would have much of a problem. I would speak English with them – very slowly if necessary– and I would use a lot of actions to explain what I wanted to say. If there was a problem with a room number or a price, I would write it down for them. I'm sure I'd be able to make myself understood. I'm very friendly and professional, so I'd have no problem making customers happy.

Interviewer OK. Can you tell me a little more about your experience in Playa del Carmen? What were your duties there?

Applicant Well, I was assistant receptionist there, which meant that I had to deal with the guests who were checking into and checking out of the hotel. I didn't have to make phone reservations – the head receptionist dealt with that. I read on your website that you only have one receptionist on the desk at any one time. Is that right?

Interviewer Yes, we're just a small hotel, so you would have to deal with guests in person and on the phone. Would that be a problem for you?

Applicant No, not at all. I mean, I haven't used a reservations program before, but I'm sure I'd pick it up really quickly. I'm very good with computers.

Interviewer Yes, the program is very easy. So, Mr. Bridges. Why do you think I should hire you and not somebody else?

Applicant Well, I think I have the right skills for the job. I'm a very reliable and efficient person, and I've had some experience in the field. I can also use my language skills to communicate with the foreign guests. The position is for a limited amount of time, which suits us both. Basically, I think that I'm perfect for the job and the job is perfect for me.

Interviewer That's fine, Mr. Bridges. One last question: When can you start?

1 B))

Host On today's program we're going to talk about superstitions. Elena, where do superstitions come from?

Elena Well, the definition of a superstition is "an irrational belief" and we have to go back hundreds of years to find an explanation of their existence. Sometimes the reason behind a superstition is even more bizarre than the superstition it tries to explain. Take the case of the black cat for example. Most people know that it's supposed to be a sign of bad luck if a black cat walks in front of you, but they probably can't tell you why. Well, the reason is that in the Middle Ages, black cats became associated with witches and they were said to possess evil spirits, so obviously people thought that if a black cat crossed your path that this was not very good news at all.

Host So the black cat superstition has been with us for a long time?

Elena Yes, but not as long as the idea that we shouldn't walk under ladders.

Apart from the practical reasons for not doing this – obviously somebody might drop some paint on your head while you are walking underneath – there is a more mysterious explanation that goes right back to ancient Egypt. The shape of a triangle was sacred to the Egyptians and it was considered very bad luck to, as it were, break the "power" of this shape. People believed that if you walked under a ladder, the power of the triangle would break and you would lose your protection against bad luck.

Host Are there any superstitions about good luck?

Elena Yes, there are. You know how people often touch wood or knock on wood when they're talking about something they hope will or won't happen in the future?

Host Yes, in fact I often do it myself.

Elena Well, in the Middle Ages people used to knock on trees to call the good spirits to protect them against misfortune. So that's where that superstition comes from.

Host We have time for one more.

Elena Well, in fact I'd say that the most common superstition concerning good luck is the habit we have of saying "Bless you" when someone sneezes. Again, this dates back to the Middle Ages when the Great Plague – which was a terrible infectious illness – was sweeping through Europe. Most people who caught the plague died and one of the first symptoms was sneezing. When sufferers began sneezing violently, it was considered a sign that they might be going to die and so the Pope passed a law in Rome requiring people to bless the person who was sneezing.

Host I never knew that. Elena, thank you so much for coming on the show. Coming up next time we have …

2 A)))

Speaker 1 Last summer, I was sitting in my yard enjoying the sun, when I heard my next door neighbor suddenly cry out. Mrs. Thomas is 93 years old and she lives alone, so I raced over to her house to see what was wrong. The kitchen door was open, so I went in and found her on her knees with her head resting on the table. She'd fallen and cut her head and there was blood everywhere. I grabbed a towel, folded it up, and pressed it onto the wound to stop the bleeding. Then I called an ambulance. She had to have stitches when she got to the hospital and they kept her in the hospital that night for observation, but she went home the next day.

Speaker 2 The only time I've ever had to use first aid was on a skiing trip to Canada. I'd gone with a few friends, and we were having a great time until disaster struck. One of my more adventurous friends was skiing down one of those slopes that is really only for experts and he suddenly lost control and crashed into a tree. By the time we reached him, he was in a lot of pain and his leg was at a really strange angle. The only thing we could do was to put snow around his leg to stop the pain and call an ambulance to take him to the hospital for an x-ray. In fact, his leg was broken in three places.

Speaker 3 I had a bit of a scare once when I was out with a friend walking our dogs. My friend, Rosie, suddenly fell and hit her head on the ground. She lost consciousness almost immediately. We were in the middle of nowhere, and I knew the emergency responders would take a long time to find us. Anyway, after calling 911, I lay Rosie on her side to make sure she was able to breathe. Then I lay down next to her and put our coats over us to keep us warm. When the paramedics arrived, they took Rosie straight to the hospital. She was fine in the end, but I found the whole thing really scary.

Speaker 4 A few years ago I remember I was playing soccer in the park with some friends and I suddenly had a terrible nosebleed. The blood was just pouring from my nose. I tried stuffing my nose with tissues, but it didn't make any difference. One of my friends told me to press ice on my face, but of course, we didn't have any ice there. Then another friend told me to pinch the soft part of my nose just under the bridge and eventually it would stop. I didn't really believe him, but I tried it and it worked!

Speaker 5 My friends and I were having a barbecue at my house when it happened. My friend Diane suddenly started coughing and excused herself from the table. Her boyfriend, Martin, went after her and we didn't think anything more of it until we heard Martin shouting for help because Diane couldn't breathe. By this time, she was turning blue, and she was clutching at her throat. I told Martin to call an ambulance, and then I hit Diane hard on the back several times. Suddenly an enormous piece of meat shot out of her mouth, and she could breathe again. We were all really shocked when it was over, especially Diane.

2 B)))

Host Hello, and welcome to the program. Today, we're talking about old age and we've asked our listeners to send in their questions. As usual, we have our expert, Laura, here in the studio with me to answer those questions. Hello, Laura.

Laura Good morning.

Host Are you ready for the first question, Laura?

Laura Yes, Bob.

Host OK then. It's from Maggie in Nashville. Maggie says: why are old people always so miserable?

Laura Well, I'm glad Maggie asked that question, Bob. The elderly have a terrible reputation for being miserable, but we've found out that it isn't actually true. According to our research, older people tend to be happier than young people. This is because they don't have so many things to worry about. Their children have left home and so they can enjoy the freedom this brings with it. So, Maggie, just to set the record straight, old people aren't miserable!

Host Thanks for clearing that up for us, Laura. Onto the next question – it's from John in New Haven. John asks: Is there a typical age when people start getting sick?

Laura That's an interesting one. Many people think that people are programmed to get sick when they get old because of something in their genes, but this isn't true. People get sick if they have an unhealthy lifestyle. If you've taken care of yourself over the years, exercising enough and eating the right food for example, then chances are that you'll be healthy in your old age. So, no John, there isn't a typical age when you start getting sick. It depends, really, on how well you cared for yourself when you were younger.

Host OK. Here's another question for you, Laura. This one is from Heather in New Orleans. She says: Old age must be really boring. People have been working hard all their lives and then suddenly they're expected to sit back and do nothing. How do they cope?

Laura That's another good question, Bob. And now that people are living longer, retirement can last for 30 years or more. But there are plenty of things you can do to fill up your time. You can do part-time work or volunteer work – you can even start a completely different career if you want to. And then, of course, there might be grandchildren to lend a hand with. So, Heather, old age doesn't have to be boring – in fact, some elderly people find that they are almost as busy when they retire as they were when they were working full-time!

Host I hope that answers your question, Heather. Let's look at another one. Richard from Portland is concerned about the issue of overpopulation. He asks: Will there be enough resources on the planet if everybody lives until they are 100?

Laura First of all, Richard, it isn't "everybody" who lives until they're 100; it's only people in the developed world. And the elderly in the developed world are a relatively small percentage of the global population. The increase in population is caused by the high birth rate in developing countries. And, sadly, many of these children never reach old age. So the question of having enough resources relates more to the population explosion in those countries, really, and not on the longer life expectancy in the West.

Host Alright. Now we have time for one more question. Jessie from Dallas asks: Do the elderly have a problem with loneliness?

Laura The thing you have to bear in mind here is that a lot of people today are living longer. This means that there will be a whole group of people just like you when you get old.

The important thing is for you to accept your age, and other people will accept you. There really is no reason to be lonely.

Host And that's very good news for all of us. Laura, thank you for joining us today.

Laura My pleasure.

3 A))

Interviewer Debbie, can you tell us about an exciting trip you've taken?

Debbie Sure. This happened a long time ago when I was working in Paris. I had a friend who was living in Palau at the time and I decided I'd like to go and visit him. Do you know where Palau is?

Interviewer Um, no. Sorry, I don't. Where is it?

Debbie Well, it's actually the Republic of Palau and it's made up of about 250 islands in the western part of the Pacific Ocean. It's about 600 miles east of the Philippines, if that helps.

Interviewer Ah, OK. I know where that is. So how did you get there?

Debbie Well, that was a problem. I went to a travel agent in Paris and the woman I spoke to told me that the trip wasn't going to be easy. First, I would have to fly to Hong Kong, then to Manila in the Philippines, and from there on to Palau.

Interviewer So, what was the problem?

Debbie Well, this was before the age of flight reservation systems. The travel agent could sell me the ticket for the Paris–Hong Kong flight, but she couldn't book any of the other flights because she had no contact with the airlines.

Interviewer So, what did you do?

Debbie I bought the ticket for Hong Kong and then the travel agent gave me the address of the airline that would take me on to Manila. The idea was that I'd fly to Hong Kong, find the offices of the airline, buy my ticket to Manila, and ask about the flights to Palau.

Interviewer Wow! What an adventure! So, is that what you did?

Debbie Yes. I didn't think anything of it at the time, you know, I was young, and it was the kind of thing that people did in the past. If you wanted to go somewhere a little bit different, you had to find your own way there.

Interviewer What happened when you got to Hong Kong?

Debbie It didn't take me long to find the offices of the airline, because they were in the airport. When they opened, I bought my ticket to Manila and asked them about the flight to Palau. And that was when the fun started.

Interviewer What do you mean?

Debbie Well, they told me that the flight from Manila to Palau only stopped in Manila to pick up cargo. The plane wasn't authorized to pick up passengers.

Interviewer Oh. That wasn't good news.

Debbie No, it wasn't. Apparently, passengers could get on the plane at all of the other stops except in Manila. I have no idea why.

Interviewer So what did you do?

Debbie Well, they said that the only thing I could do was to fly to Manila, find the plane and talk to the pilot. If the pilot agreed to take me, then I could fly to Palau.

Interviewer Don't tell me that's what you did!

Debbie Well, actually, it is. I took my flight to Manila and hung around for a while waiting for the plane to Palau. When it came in, I asked the flight attendant if I could speak to the pilot. It was a tiny plane, and there were only about 13 passengers on it, but they had their very own flight attendant.

Interviewer And what did she say?

Debbie Actually, she seemed pretty excited about me speaking English. I found out why when she introduced me to the pilot – he was Australian! He was amused by my adventure and agreed immediately to take me on to Palau.

Interviewer You were so lucky!

Debbie Yes, I know. But the best thing was that my friend was at the airport to meet me when I landed. I hadn't told him when I'd be getting there – nobody had a cell phone then either – but he'd just dropped by on his way home from work to see if I was there.

Interviewer That's amazing!

Debbie Absolutely. I don't think I'll ever forget that trip.

Interviewer I'm not surprised!

3 B))

Speaker 1 I only ever have time to read when I'm on vacation, but it's something that I really look forward to. I always make a point of picking up two or three of the latest best sellers from my local book store. When I'm away, I take my book with me to the beach or down to the pool, and then I spend all day lying in the sun, reading. What better way to relax and completely disconnect from life back home?

Speaker 2 I spend a lot of time reading when I'm commuting to and from my job. The trip takes about an hour and a half each way, first on the train and then on the subway. I usually manage to get a seat on the train because it's one of the first stops. As soon as I sit down, I take out my e-reader, and fall into the latest novel I'm reading. I'm a big fan of historical novels, and I get through at least one book a week.

Speaker 3 I'm studying civil engineering in college, so I have to do a lot of reading, though none of it is for pleasure. At the start of the semester, they gave us a booklist as long as my arm, but I haven't read all the books on it yet. Apart from academic books, I read a lot on the Internet. There are a lot of web pages related to my studies, some of them better than others. I do most of my reading in my room, although I sometimes go to the library.

Speaker 4 This may sound strange, but I do most of my reading when I'm at the gym! Actually, for me it's more of a case of listening than reading because I always take an audio book with me. I download the book onto my MP3 player so that I can listen to it while I'm on a spin bike. I do a workout that is 50 minutes to an hour long, so my audio book helps me pass the time. I'm really into crime fiction, so I usually listen to detective stories.

Speaker 5 I used to read a lot, but now I can't, because I have two small children who take up all my time. The only reading I do these days are children's stories. My sons are three and five, and neither of them will go to sleep without their bedtime story. Every night, it's the same routine – bath, dinner, story – the only thing that changes is whose bed we lie on! Their favorite is *The Hungry Caterpillar*, but I like the Doctor Seuss stories.

4 A))

And our next story takes us to Australia, where an extreme sports enthusiast had a lucky escape today. Thirty-five-year-old Ewa Wisnierska from Germany was preparing for the World Paragliding Championships when she saw a massive thunderstorm coming toward her. The storm appeared out of nowhere while she was paragliding over Manila, in New South Wales, Australia. She tried to avoid it, but, because paragliders have no engine, she could not go fast enough to get away from it. When the storm caught up with her, it lifted her up into the air. She told an Australian radio station that the strong winds blew her up in the air "like a leaf from a tree."

The storm took just under 15 minutes to carry the paraglider from a height of 2,460 feet to an estimated height of 6 miles. During the ascent, the temperature dropped to around minus 58 degrees Fahrenheit and

Ms. Wisnierska witnessed hailstones the size of oranges. Here's how Ewa describes her experience: "I was shaking all the time. The last thing I remember it was dark. I could hear lightning all around me." She was sucked up so high that eventually she lost consciousness, but her paraglider continued flying. The whole ordeal was recorded by the GPS system and radio that was attached to her equipment.

Luckily for Ms. Wisnierska, she was only unconscious for about half an hour. When she came to, she had descended to around 4 miles and she was covered in ice. She managed to take control of her paraglider and succeeded in descending by herself. She told reporters later that she felt like an astronaut as she was returning to the ground. "I could see the Earth coming, like *Apollo* 13." She eventually landed about 200 feet from the site where she had taken off. She had ice in her flying suit and frostbite on her face from the extremely low temperatures she had experienced. As soon as she reached the ground, she was taken to the hospital for observation, but she was released an hour later.

The competition organizers stressed how lucky Ms. Wisnierska had been to regain consciousness while she was up in the air. The body of another Chinese paraglider was found later in the day, about 260 feet from where he had taken off. Forty-two-year-old He Zhongpin from China had been caught up in the same storm as the German woman, but he had not survived the ordeal. Apparently, he had died from extreme cold and a lack of oxygen.

4 B))

Host And I'd like to welcome Andy Evans, the Director of Extreme Sports United to the program today. Andy, your specialty is bungee jumping, isn't it?

Andy Yes, it is.

Host Can you tell us something about bungee jumping? Whose idea was it?

Andy Well, bungee jumping has been around for centuries, but it wasn't discovered in the West until relatively recently. It originated on the South Pacific island of Vanuatu, where young men known as "land divers" used to perform the ritual of jumping from tall wooden platforms with vines tied to their ankles.

Host And when did "land diving" actually become a sport?

Andy Well, the first modern bungee jump happened about 20 years later in Bristol in the UK. A man named Chris Baker used

a kind of elastic rope to make a bungee – that's the name of the rope – and four members of the Dangerous Sports Club made a jump from the Clifton Suspension Bridge on April 1, 1979. They were arrested almost immediately afterward, but people continued jumping off bridges, especially in the US. For example, people did bungee jumps from the Golden Gate Bridge in San Francisco. In fact, some of these jumps were sponsored by American TV and so this brought the concept of bungee jumping to the public eye and then, of course, a lot of people wanted to try it themselves.

Host How dangerous is bungee jumping? I mean, have people been killed while they were bungee jumping?

Andy Actually, there have been relatively few fatalities considering the number of successful jumps that have taken place. By far the most important thing is to make sure the bungee is the right length. The most common cause of death is using a bungee that is too long, but in most cases the calculations and fittings are double-checked before each jump.

Host How does it actually feel doing a bungee jump?

Andy Well, many people say they love the feeling of falling so fast, but personally, the part I really like best is when the bungee reaches its full extent and then you fly upward again. You just can't beat the feeling of flying back up after you've almost hit the ground.

5 A))

OK, if I can have your attention, please. Good morning, everybody. My name's Sam, I'm a firefighter, and I'm here today to give you some tips on how to prevent house fires. I'll also be telling you the best way of getting out of a fire, if you ever happen to be trapped in one.

Most fires in the home happen while people are sleeping. One of the most important steps you can take to protect your family is to install a smoke alarm on each floor of your house. Once you've got your smoke alarm installed and working, you should make an escape plan with your family to make sure everyone knows how to get out.

Of course, there are other precautions you can take. The most common causes of fatal fires in the home are tobacco and smoking products, so it's best to avoid smoking in the bedroom. It's also important to keep matches and lighters out of reach of children, preferably in a locked cabinet. Never leave food that's cooking unattended, especially hot oil if you're frying.

As well as preventing fires in the home, you also need to know what to do if a fire does break out. If you get trapped in your home by smoke or flames, close all doors, and stuff towels or clothing under the doors to keep smoke out. Cover your nose and mouth with a damp cloth to protect your lungs. If you have to escape through a smoky area, remember that cleaner air is always nearer the floor, so you'll need to crawl out on all fours.

Finally, and very importantly, if a fire breaks out, do not try to rescue pets or possessions. There isn't time to do this – you must get out as soon as possible. Once you have gotten out, do not go back in for any reason. Firefighters have a better chance of rescuing people who are trapped than you do.

OK, any questions?

5 B))

Daniel So what annoys you about my family?

Ana Are you really sure you want to talk about this?

Daniel Sure, why not? What's the problem? They're not that bad, are they?

Ana No, of course not, but I have a different perspective, don't you think?

Daniel Oh, come on! I'd really like to know what you think.

Ana Well, all right then.

Daniel What about my mom?

Ana Well, I think she's really nice…

Daniel But…

Ana But she drives me crazy when I'm cooking. I mean, if she wants to help, that's great, but I wish she wouldn't keep complaining that my cabinets aren't organized. I'm very happy with my house and the way it looks, so I wish she wouldn't criticize all the time!

Daniel Well, I don't think she's that bad, I mean, I think she just wants to help…

Ana Yes, and I'm grateful for her help, but not for her comments, OK? That's just how I feel, all right?

Daniel OK. OK. What about Dad?

Ana Well, he's not really interested in anyone else, is he? I mean, if he's happy then that's fine, and if he isn't, well, everyone else has to make sure that he's all right.

Daniel I don't think that's very fair. He's not well. And he gets tired quickly and…

Ana You asked me to tell you what I think, so I'm telling you, OK? I just don't think it's right that we all have to go running around after your dad when there are other people to think about. I mean, there are the kids to worry about, too. OK, it's your turn now.

Daniel What?

Ana To tell me about my family.

Daniel Well, after what you said I don't know where to start! Well, really, your mom can be pretty unbearable. In fact, I've been meaning to…

6 A)))

Host … and continuing our overview of what's on and where this week, we're going to move on to movies. Judith is here to tell us about a documentary that is showing at the independent movie theater next week. Judith?

Judith Yes, Robert. The documentary is called *Alive Inside* and it was made by Michael Rossalto Bennett, an alternative US filmmaker. The documentary explores the positive effect that music can have on patients suffering from Alzheimer's disease. It follows the progress of a social worker named Dan Cohen and his plan to introduce music in nursing homes in New York where people with Alzheimer's are being taken care of.

Host How interesting. Tell us more.

Judith In the documentary, we see how he visits the nursing homes and meets some of the patients. What he does is to create a personalized playlist for the patients, which they can listen to on an MP3 player or an iPod. He finds out which songs to include by interviewing each patient's family. By creating the playlist, he hopes that the patients will be able to travel back to the time to when they heard the songs and maybe it will even help them remember important events in their past.

Host And does it work?

Judith Well, I'm giving away some of the story here, but yes, yes it does work. Cohen's biggest success story is a man named Henry. Maybe you've seen the clip about Henry on YouTube?

Host No, I haven't. What is it?

Judith Oh, OK. Well, Henry is special because of the astonishing transformation that happens to him when he listens to his playlist for the first time. When we first see him, he is sitting in his chair with his head down and he's barely capable of answering questions, except with a monosyllabic "yes" or "no." But when he's given his headphones, he turns into a completely different person. His eyes open wide, his face lights up, and he starts moving to the music. He can even answer questions about the song he's listening to. It's actually very emotional watching his reaction, which is probably why millions of people have seen that video clip I mentioned.

Host It sounds like an amazing story, Judith. But do the playlists work for everybody?

Judith They seem to work for most people, yes. And they have had a much wider effect than helping only individuals. At first, Cohen was worried that the iPods might isolate the patients as each one would be listening to his or her own set. But, in fact, the playlists are encouraging them to socialize. The staff members in all four of the nursing homes he worked with in New York reported that the music was helping the residents to talk to each other more. The patients would ask each other questions about the music, and in some cases, they wanted to share the different songs.

Host What effect has Cohen's work had on other nursing homes across the country?

Judith It's too early to say what will happen in nursing homes across the country, but in New York, there have definitely been some changes. One of the greatest obstacles to the plan is the cost. MP3 players aren't cheap, and providing one for every patient in each nursing home would just be too expensive. But Cohen is trying to get around this problem by asking people to donate any old MP3 players or iPods that they may have lying at home at the back of a drawer.

Host Well, this sounds like a really worthwhile project, Judith. But what about the film? Would you recommend it?

Judith Yes, definitely – especially if someone in your family suffers from Alzheimer's. You'll find it a great comfort.

Host Thanks, Judith, for your recommendation. And just to remind you of the name of that documentary, it's *Alive Inside*, and it's showing at the independent movie theater from Monday to Saturday next week. And now it's time to look at what's on at the theater…

6 B)))

Host Hello, and welcome to the program. Now, we all know that the amount of sleep you get each night can affect your work and your ability to interact with others. Health specialists say that the amount of sleep the average person needs is between seven and nine hours per night. Some new research suggests that diet plays an important role in whether we get a good night of sleep or not. Dietician Richard Vickers is here with us in the studio to tell us more. Good morning, Richard, and welcome to the program.

Richard Hello, Holly.

Host So, Richard, we all know that coffee tends to keep us awake at night. What else should we avoid at dinner time?

Richard Well, actually, Holly, it isn't only coffee that can disturb sleep; it is any food or beverage that contains caffeine, for example chocolate, or tea, or many soft drinks. Of course, caffeine doesn't affect everybody in the same way, but if you are sensitive to it, you should avoid it in the afternoon and in the evening. That way, it won't keep you awake at night.

Host Is there anything else that can potentially stop us sleeping?

Richard Yes, there is. Your sleep can be disturbed if your dinner has a high fat content. The body takes a long time to digest fat, which can make you feel very uncomfortable when you go to bed. People who have extra butter on their bread or heavy cream with their dessert often complain of heartburn or indigestion when they go to bed.

Host That makes sense. So, does it make a difference what time you have dinner compared to the time you go to bed?

Richard Yes, it does. People who suffer from heartburn or indigestion should avoid eating late at all costs. Lying down with a full stomach makes it much more difficult for the body to digest food, causing discomfort and sometimes pain. In fact, eating late can affect all kinds of people, so, in general, I wouldn't recommend it. The same can be said of the quantity you have. Heavy meals should be consumed at lunch time, and you should aim to be eating a light snack in the evening. This will fill your stomach so that you aren't hungry when you go to bed, but it won't make you feel so full that you can't sleep.

Host Richard, we've talked about the amount of food we should and shouldn't eat. What about liquids?

Richard Well, for a good night of sleep, you're obviously better off drinking water with your dinner. But you shouldn't drink too much of that, either. Don't drink too much at dinner time or after dinner, or your sleep will be disrupted because you will have to go to the bathroom during the night.

Host OK. So much for what we shouldn't do. Is there anything that will actually help us go to sleep at night?

Richard Yes, there is – milk. Milk contains a special substance that affects the way that certain hormones in the brain work. One of these hormones is serotonin, which helps us fall asleep. This is why members of the older generation often have a hot, milky drink before they go to bed.

Host Is there anything else that can help?

Richard Yes, there's an herb called valerian, which seems to work well. Research has shown that substances in the root of the valerian plant relax the central nervous system and the muscles. You can take it in liquid or tablet form or you can make a tea out of it. People who have used valerian have said that it has helped them fall asleep quicker and it has given them a deep and satisfying rest.

Host It sounds like valerian might be the answer, then. I'm afraid that's all we have time for today, Richard. Thank you so much for joining us.

Richard My pleasure.

7 A)))

Speaker 1 My husband and I had just been food shopping, and we were having an argument about something – how much money we'd spent, or why we'd bought one particular item of food – I don't know. Anyway, the argument continued into the kitchen, and while we were putting all the food away, my husband kept on banging his hand on the table every time he made a point, but he didn't realize that, without thinking about it, he had picked up one of those little plastic yogurt cups. Suddenly, he hit the table and there was yogurt everywhere – on the table, on the floor, on the ceiling, on the walls … and on him. We both just burst out laughing … and that was the end of the argument.

Speaker 2 I had an argument with my dad once over a pair of sneakers. We were in the mall when I saw a really nice pair of DC sneakers in a store window. I pointed them out to my dad, but he'd never heard of the brand DC, and so he said that they must've been made by another designer brand called Dolce and Gabbana – DG. No matter how hard I tried, I couldn't convince him that the sneakers were DC and not DG. In the end, he said he'd buy them for me if I was right. So we went into the store to ask about the sneakers. The salesperson said, "You mean the DC ones?" proving that I had been right all along. You should have seen my dad's face!

Speaker 3 I was with my girlfriend one night and we'd decided to go to a fast food restaurant to get some burgers to go. Anyway, we started arguing about something in the car on the way – I don't know what started it, but I remember getting pretty angry. The argument continued while we parked, while we were standing in line, while we were ordering, while we were paying, and while we were going home. We were concentrating so much on the argument that we didn't realize that we hadn't picked up the food. We were still arguing in the car, when suddenly my girlfriend said, "Where are the hamburgers?" Then, of course, we had to drive back to the restaurant to get the food!

Speaker 4 This happened when I was little. I was in the kitchen with my sister when my parents started having an argument. My dad was starting to shout when my older brother came in – he must've been about 16 at the time, but he was already taller than my dad. My brother tried to get my dad to calm down, but my dad wasn't listening. In the end, my brother said to him, "OK. You're going to your room." He picked him up, put him over his shoulder, and started taking him upstairs. This broke the tension immediately, and everyone started laughing – including my dad. Honestly, if you could have seen him, holding onto the stair rail, trying to stop my brother from getting him upstairs! It's one of the funniest things I've ever seen!

Speaker 5 This happened a couple of years ago while I was at work – I work at one of those helpline call centers where people call if they have a problem with their Internet connections. Well, anyway, this woman called and she was absolutely furious because she couldn't get her Internet to work. She was so angry, that she was just screaming into the phone at me. Suddenly, there was a break in the conversation, and I said to her, "So, what's the weather like up there where you live?" I don't know what came over me, but those were the words that came out of my mouth. And it worked! The woman was so shocked that she stopped shouting and answered my question. After that, we were able to have a reasonably civil conversation, and I managed to solve her problem for her.

7 B)))

Host Hello and welcome to the program. Today, we're trying to answer the question: What makes a good actor? Our next guest is drama teacher Nicholas Whitby. He's going to tell us a little bit about method acting. Hello Nicholas, and welcome to the show.

Nicholas Hello, Lily.

Host So, Nicholas, what exactly is method acting?

Nicholas Well, method acting is the technique that actors use to create in themselves the thoughts and feelings of their characters. Different actors use different techniques to do this, but the original technique involves doing a series of sense memory exercises.

Host Sense memory? What's that?

Nicholas Well, a memory is a situation that you have a recollection of, right? Well a sense memory is the recollection of the sensations you experienced during that situation. Method actors use this sense memory to help them recreate a particular emotion in front of the camera. They have to do exercises to make this work effectively.

Host What kind of exercises?

Nicholas Well, what most of them do is to focus on the particular situation in the past until the sensations they experienced come back to them. They do this in sessions of 15 minutes or so, until they can reproduce their feelings automatically. For example, if a movie is set in the North Pole, the actor needs to show that he is really cold. So he does his sense memory exercise to help him remember a time when he experienced intense cold. Then he can convince the audience that he is really cold.

Host Do all actors do these sense memory exercises?

Nicholas No, they don't, Lily. Method acting can mean the difference between an Oscar-winning actor and an ordinary actor. Going back to our scene in the North Pole, an ordinary actor would indicate the cold by shivering, wrapping his arms around himself and blowing into his freezing hands. He wouldn't actually be feeling the cold, which would mean that the audience probably wouldn't feel it either.

Host Talking of Oscar winners, Nicholas, tell us about some of the best method actors.

Nicholas Well, let's look at the men first. One actor who goes even further than the use of sense memory is three-time Oscar winner Daniel Day-Lewis. Day-Lewis is known for immersing himself in every role he plays. In *My Left Foot*, he played the severely disabled Irish writer, Christy Brown. During filming, the crew had to feed him in his wheelchair, and he learned to put a record onto a record player with his foot. A couple of years later, he spent several months living in the wild in preparation for another movie, *Last of the Mohicans*. And in 2012's *Lincoln*, he walked and talked like Abraham Lincoln the whole of the time that the movie was being shot.

Host What about female actors, Nicholas?

Nicholas Probably the best example of a female actor who made a superhuman effort to enter her part is Charlize Theron in the movie *Monster*. Before *Monster* came out, we were used to seeing Ms. Theron playing superficial female parts requiring a woman with a pretty face. Which is what made her transformation into the serial killer in *Monster* so shocking. Ms. Theron put on nearly 30 pounds in order to play the role, and anybody who has seen the movie will tell you, she is one of the scariest murderers who has ever hit the big screen. Not surprisingly, she won the Oscar for Best Actress that year.

Host Yes, I remember that one. And I remember Charlize Theron being terribly convincing. Thank you for joining us, Nicholas, and explaining method acting to us. Next on the program we're going to talk about …

8 A))

Speaker 1 This was something that happened to a friend of mine. It was very late, about eleven thirty, and he was walking home from work. While he was going through the park, this guy came up to him and told him to give him all his money, which he did. Then the guy asked him for his cell phone, but my friend refused to give it to him, so the guy hit him really hard and knocked him to the ground, breaking his arm. By the time my friend got to the hospital he was in terrible pain, and later the doctors told him he'd been really lucky. It just shows it's better not to try to be brave if something like that happens to you.

Speaker 2 I don't know why, but I always seem to have my wallet stolen when I'm abroad. I guess it's because I'm speaking English and I probably look like a tourist, or something. The last time, I was in a very touristy street in the center of town, but luckily I wasn't carrying much in my wallet, just a few dollars. I've gotten so used to it now that I always take my personal documents out of my wallet and leave them in the hotel. That way, if I'm robbed, I only lose a little bit of money.

Speaker 3 I did something really stupid once. I was traveling home by train and I was really tired, so I fell asleep. Unfortunately, I left my bag with all my things in it on the floor, and I didn't notice when someone took it. I realized what had happened when I woke up and as soon as the train arrived in the station I went right to the police. Amazingly, the police found my bag, but of course my wallet, my phone, and my MP3 player were all missing. I can't believe I was so stupid!

Speaker 4 My mom was on vacation once with a group of friends. They were walking back to their beach condo when a thief tried to grab one of the women's

bags. But she didn't let go and started screaming. The other women started screaming too and all of them started hitting him. He ran away without the bag and the group went into a cafe where the people had seen what had happened and all cheered for them. After that, they decided to get a taxi back to the beach condo.

Speaker 5 I was sitting in a coffee shop once when I saw someone take one of the other customer's bags. The thief was with a friend on a motorcycle. The two of them drove up outside the cafe together and then one of them jumped off and ran inside. He grabbed the first bag he came across and then ran back out of the door again. He jumped onto the back of the motorcycle and the two of them rode off. It all happened so fast that nobody had a chance to react.

8 B))

Host Hello and welcome to the show. On today's program we're looking at famous media mistakes. Journalist Simon Bennett is here in the studio with me and he's going to tell us about a rather memorable weather forecast. Good morning, Simon.

Simon Hello, Silvia.

Host Simon, tell us what happened.

Simon Well, this happened back in October 1987. The forecaster of that particular weather broadcast was Michael Fish – a familiar face in most British households because he'd been forecasting the weather for over thirty years. During the program, Michael referred to a phone call a woman had made to the BBC. Apparently, the woman had asked if there was going to be a hurricane. Michael laughed and said, "If the lady is watching, don't worry, there isn't going to be a hurricane." And nobody thought anything more about it until later on that night.

Host That's right, there was a terrible storm, wasn't there?

Simon Yes, there was. That night, a huge storm hit southern England. To be absolutely accurate, it wasn't actually a hurricane, because hurricanes have to form in tropical areas to be called by that name. But there certainly was a terrible storm that night with winds of up to 110 miles per hour. These wind speeds are typical of hurricanes, which is why there is some confusion about what to call the storm.

Host So, what kind of damage did it cause?

Simon The storm killed 18 people and many more were injured – mainly by falling trees. And it caused billions of dollars worth of damage. Millions of homes were left without power, because trees had fallen on power lines. Transportation in the southern part of the country was severely disrupted because fallen trees had blocked the roads and railways. In total, about 15 million trees fell down that night and the scene the next morning was complete chaos. It was the worst storm to hit the UK in living memory.

Host What happened to Michael Fish after that?

Simon A lot of people blamed him for all the damage because he hadn't warned them about the storm. Worse still, he had said that there wasn't going to be a storm at all. Since then, he has tried several times to make excuses for his words, but deep down, nobody believes him. Michael Fish has gone down in history as the forecaster who failed to predict a hurricane. In fact, twenty-five years after the event, he appeared in the opening ceremony of the 2012 London Olympic Games giving a repeat performance of his famous broadcast.

Host You can see a video of the original broadcast on YouTube as well, can't you, Simon?

Simon Yes, that's right.

Host And now it's time for our weather broadcast – let's hope we don't make the same mistake as Michael Fish! Simon Bennett, thank you so much for joining us.

Simon My pleasure.

Weatherman Thanks, Sylvia. So a pretty bright start for most of us this morning, temperatures already around the 60-degree mark …

9 A))

Host And now it's time for the part of the program when we ask our listeners to give us their opinion about a story that has been in the news recently. And today, we're looking at the story of the New Jersey man who bought a lottery ticket with a pool of five coworkers in November of 2009 and cashed it, but didn't share it. He kept all the money for himself. Just in case you haven't heard, Americo Lopes, a construction worker, bought a Mega Millions lottery ticket to share with his coworkers. When Mr. Lopes discovered the ticket had won a prize, he took it to the lottery office and cashed it for the prize money, which was more than $38.5 million. Mr. Lopes didn't tell anyone he had won the lottery and quit his job claiming he needed foot surgery. Several months later Mr. Lopes told a friend about his winning ticket. When his coworkers discovered he'd won the lottery, they took him to court where the jury decided that Mr. Lopes would have to split his winnings with five coworkers. We want to know what you think about all this. Who do you think should get the prize money– all of the coworkers in the lottery pool or just Mr. Lopes? The number to call is 1-800-555-5362, and the lines have just opened. I'll say that number again for you, it's 1-800-555-5362. And here's our first caller. Andrew from Trenton, what do you think?

Caller 1 Well, I think Mr. Lopes should keep all the money. Maybe he bought a lottery ticket with his own money in addition to getting one for his lottery pool. You never know. Also, there's no law against keeping the information about winning the lottery to yourself. Maybe he's a very private person and he doesn't like sharing information about his life.

Host Thank you for calling, Andrew. And now we have Mara from Boise on the line. Mara, do you agree with Andrew?

Caller 2 No, I don't. Not at all. Even if that man bought the lottery ticket with his own money, he should still share it with his coworkers. They had a deal. If the ticket was worth money, then all the coworkers should have a share. If Mr. Lopes didn't want to share the money, he never should have joined a lottery pool in the first place. Am I shocked that he tried to keep all the money to himself? No, I'm not. Money does terrible things to people!

Host Thanks for that, Mara. And our next caller is … hold on a moment … yes, it's Roger from Binghamton. What do you think, Roger?

Caller 3 Well, I was brought up to understand that if I kept an object or money that belonged to other people, I would be stealing. I can't understand why there's so much confusion here. Morally, the man should have told his coworkers about the ticket immediately after he learned it was a winner. The jury was right to make Mr. Lopes share the money with his coworkers. It wasn't his to keep to himself in the first place.

Host Thank you for calling, Roger. And now it's Beth's turn. Beth's from Tucson. Tell us what you think, Beth.

Caller 4 Yes, the last caller said the man had a moral obligation to share the lottery ticket, but in fact, he had a legal obligation to do so, too. The group didn't keep written records of the tickets they bought together. Because of this Mr. Lopes

can't prove one way or the other that the winning ticket was his alone. Legally, this casts doubt on Mr. Lopes's claims.

Host Thanks for explaining the legal aspects of the case to us, Beth. And we have time for one more caller. It's Carlos from Long Island. Carlos, what's your opinion?

Caller 5 Well, I have some sympathy for Mr. Lopes, you know. He's the one who actually bought the ticket and when he discovered that it had won a prize, he cashed it. Did anyone in the lottery pool ask if the ticket was a winner? Did they ask Mr. Lopes what the numbers on the tickets were? The point is that the coworkers were just as responsible for knowing the ticket information as Mr. Lopes was.

Host Thank you for calling, Carlos. We'll be back with some more views in a moment, but first it's time for the news …

9 B))

Speaker 1 My favorite city is on the East Coast of the United States on the banks of the Potomac River. It's named in honor of the first president of the United States, and it's well known for its many historical monuments such as the Lincoln Memorial, the Vietnam Veterans Memorial, and the Jefferson Memorial. It also has the world's largest museum— The Smithsonian Institution. The best time of year to visit, in my opinion, is in the spring during the National Cherry Blossom Festival. Three thousand cherry trees around the city, a gift from Japan in 1912, are covered in tiny pink flowers. It's quite breathtaking.

Speaker 2 The most beautiful city I've ever visited is on the Pacific coast of Canada. It's surrounded by water on three sides, and has the Coast Mountain Range on the other. There's a large island across from the city where Canadians often go on vacation. It also has the largest urban park in North America, called Stanley Park, which has a zoo, a marine science center, and famous gardens containing native trees. It's known as one of the cities with the highest quality of life in the world.

Speaker 3 My favorite city is the capital of a South American country. It's on the banks of the Rio de la Plata and is famous for being the birthplace of tango. It's one of the world's busiest ports and the residents often refer to themselves as *Porteños*. The main square is called the Plaza de Mayo, and one of this city's streets, the Avenida 9 de Julio is said to be the widest boulevard in the world.

Although it's not in Europe, it actually feels quite European – parts of it remind me of Paris and other parts of Italy. In fact, one of the districts is called Palermo Viejo, like the capital of Sicily.

Speaker 4 I took a gap year between graduating from high school and starting college and I went traveling. I visited a lot of wonderful places, but the one I liked best was a city on the southeast coast of Australia. It's a very cosmopolitan city, full of many different cultures, and it has the best Chinatown that I've ever seen! One of the most fascinating things about it is the architecture: beautiful old buildings from the Victorian era contrast with the latest design in skyscrapers – the difference is striking. It's a fairly big city, with a lot of parks and gardens, and there are some amazing beaches nearby.

Speaker 5 I'm lucky, because my job allows me to spend one month every year working in my favorite big city. It's on the south coast of China, and I think it's amazing. It's pretty crowded, but that makes it even more exciting as far as I'm concerned. It's a real mixture of East and West; on the one hand it's an international financial center, and on the other you can find traditional old markets selling all kinds of different food. There are green parks full of people doing Tai Chi first thing in the morning, and the city has a really modern and efficient tram and metro system, so it's very easy to get around.

10 A))

Host Hello and welcome to the program. Now most people associate NASA with astronauts and rocket ships. What they don't know is that NASA research extends far beyond space flight and into our daily lives. Our special guest today is freelance science journalist, Hank Webb. He's going to tell us about some of the products invented by NASA that we use every day. Good morning, Hank.

Hank Hi, there.

Host So, Hank, where are you going to start?

Hank Well, I'm going to start with something that has saved lives in many homes all over the world: the smoke detector. In the 1970s, when NASA engineers were designing the first US space station, called *Skylab*, they realized that the astronauts would need to know if a fire had started or if there were poisonous gases in the air. The engineers teamed up with a company called the Honeywell Corporation and together they invented a special kind of smoke detector. The new model was adjustable. Astronauts could change the level of sensitivity on it so that there was never a false alarm.

Host That's fascinating. What's next?

Hank Well, the next one has changed the lives of people who need glasses. As you know, the two lenses in a pair of glasses used to be made of, well, glass. Glass lenses often broke when the glasses were dropped, so opticians started using plastic instead. Plastic doesn't break, but it does scratch easily, and scratched lenses can damage your sight. NASA solved this problem when they developed a new substance to protect the helmets worn by astronauts. The substance stops the plastic from scratching so easily. Manufacturers of glasses soon started using this new technology in their products, which is why the lenses in today's glasses are less likely to scratch than they were in the past.

Host And that's great news for all of us who wear glasses. We have time for one more, Hank.

Hank Alright. I'll tell you about the ear thermometer, then. This was developed from the infrared technology that NASA uses to measure the temperature of stars. A company called Diatek saw a need to reduce the amount of time nurses spent taking temperatures. Together with NASA, the company invented an infrared sensor that serves as the thermometer. The sensor takes your temperature by measuring the amount of heat produced inside your ear. The ear thermometers used in hospitals can take your temperature in less than two seconds.

Host Yes, and those thermometers are a vast improvement on the ones with mercury inside – I can never seem to read them. Hank Webb, thank you so much for joining us.

Hank My pleasure.

10 B)))

Host Hello and welcome to the program. Now, public speaking can be a harrowing experience at the best of times, but imagine how difficult it must be for an important person with a stammer. This is exactly the problem faced by George VI, King of England from 1936 to 1952. Now we're going to find out a little bit more about the King's condition. Good morning, Sarah.

Sarah Hello.

Host So, Sarah, do we know what caused the King's stammer?

Sarah Well, according to the leading speech therapy expert, Rosemarie Hayhow, the King's stammer developed when he was a child – everybody called him Bertie then, so I will, too. Bertie's problem was a psychological one. His father, George V, was a demanding man who would not tolerate weakness. When he saw that his second son was left-handed, he forced Bertie to write with his right hand. This is something that is often associated with stammering today.

Host Did Bertie have any other problems with his family?

Sarah Yes, with his elder brother, Edward. Edward used to laugh at Bertie when he stammered, which made his problem even worse.

Host Did Bertie ever have to speak in public?

Sarah Not usually, no. But in 1925, his father asked him to give the closing address at the British Empire Exhibition at Wembley. The speech was broadcast live to the nation, and it was a complete disaster. Bertie stammered out a few words and then the broadcast ended in silence. It was then that he realized he had to get help.

Host Who did he turn to?

Sarah Well, first of all he tried his father's doctors, whose methods were very old-fashioned. They used to make him fill his mouth with marbles and on one occasion, he nearly choked! Fortunately, his wife, Elizabeth, was able to find a different therapist for him. It was an Australian named Lionel Logue, who was actually an actor. Mr. Logue had been working as a speech therapist with soldiers who had lost their ability to speak because of the traumas of war.

Host How did Mr. Logue treat Bertie?

Sarah Well, to start with, Mr. Logue insisted on seeing Bertie in his Harley Street office. And he refused to use Bertie's official title, which was the "Duke of York." Instead, he called him "Bertie." Mr. Logue used techniques that gave Bertie more confidence. He made him sing instead of speaking; he played music to him through headphones while he was reading, so that he couldn't hear himself and become self-conscious; he even got Bertie to swear. After about ten months, the treatment seemed to be working.

Host Which was a good job, wasn't it? Because soon after that, Bertie became King of England.

Sarah That's right, Jeremy. When George V died, Bertie's brother, Edward, became King Edward VIII. But Edward wanted to marry an American woman who was divorced, which he was forbidden from doing as King. In the end, Edward abdicated and Bertie became King George VI. Which meant that he had to start speaking in public again.

Host So, what happened?

Sarah At first, the King avoided making live speeches, but by 1939 he couldn't do this any longer. On September 3rd of that year, Britain declared war on Germany and the King had to deliver the most important speech of his life.

Host So what did he do?

Sarah He asked Mr. Logue to help him. The two men went into a small room with the recording equipment and closed the door. Mr. Logue opened a window and told the King to take off his jacket. Then, he advised the King to forget everybody else and say the speech to him, as a friend.

Host Did it work?

Sarah Yes, it did. The King's delivery was calm, dignified, and measured. And at the end of the broadcast, Mr. Logue finally called him "Your Majesty."

198 Madison Avenue
New York, NY 10016 USA

Great Clarendon Street, Oxford, OX2 6DP, United Kingdom

Oxford University Press is a department of the University of Oxford.
It furthers the University's objective of excellence in research, scholarship,
and education by publishing worldwide. Oxford is a registered trade
mark of Oxford University Press in the UK and in certain other countries.

ISBN: 978 0 19 477606 6 WORKBOOK

ACKNOWLEDGEMENTS

*The authors would like to thank all the teachers and students round the world whose
feedback has helped us to shape* English File.

The authors would also like to thank: all those at Oxford University Press (both
in Oxford and around the world) and the design team who have contributed
their skills and ideas to producing this course.

*Finally very special thanks from Clive to Maria Angeles, Lucia, and Eric, and from
Christina to Cristina, for all their support and encouragement. Christina would also like
to thank her children Joaquin, Marco, and Krysia for their constant inspiration.*

The authors and publisher are grateful to those who have given permission to reproduce
the following extracts and adaptations of copyright material: p.7 Adapted extract
from "India goes bananas for 24-hour astrology" by Amrit Dhillon, www.
telegraph.co.uk, 1 April 2007 © Telegraph Media Group Limited 2007.
Reproduced by permission. p.11 Adapted extract from "Mixed messages:
Medical Myths" by Rachel C Vreeman and Aaron E Carroll, BMJ 2007; 335,
www.bmj.com, (Published 20 December 2007). Reproduced by permission
of BMJ. p.20 Reprinted by permission of Scholastic Inc. from "Questions &
Answers: A Conversation with Suzanne Collins: Author of *The Hunger Games
Trilogy*." Copyright © 2013 by Scholastic Inc. p.20 Adapted extract from "How
we work: Philip Pullman, author"; an interview with the Achuka website
www.achuka.co.uk. Reproduced by permission. p.24 Adapted extract from
"Leaving our mark" by David Chandler, MIT News Office, 16 April 2008,
reprinted by permission of MIT News Office. p.26 Adapted extract from
"Storm whips paraglider to heights of 32,000 ft" by Nick Squires, www.
telegraph.co.uk, 16 February 2007 © Telegraph Media Group Limited 2007.
Reproduced by permission. p.34 Adapted extract from TED Talk "Don't
regret regret" by Kathryn Schulz, www.ted.com. Reproduced by permission
of Kathryn Schulz. p.37 Adapted extract from "Music made me deaf" by
Phillippa Faulks, Daily Mail, 5 January 2010. Reproduced by permission of
Solo Syndication. p.41 Adapted extract from "'Don't put the duck there. It's
totally irresponsible.' Sleep-talking husband's hilarious lines become internet
sensation" by Carol Driver, Daily Mail online, 14 January 2010. Reproduced
by permission of Solo Syndication. p.47 Adapted extract from TED Talk "How
to spot a liar" by Pamela Meyer, www.ted.com. Reproduced by permission of
Pamela Meyer. p.64 Adapted extract from "The Unknown Geniuses Behind
10 Of The Most Useful Inventions Ever" by Alana Horowitz, Business Insider
Magazine, 3 March 2011. Reproduced by permission of Wright's Media., p.49
Adapted extract from "How we made: Peter Shaffer and Felicity Kendal on
Amadeus" by Anna Tims, The Guardian, 14 January 2013. Copyright Guardian
News & Media Ltd 2013. Reproduced by permission.

Sources: http://jobsearch.about.com, www.wikihow.com, www.flightcentre.
com.au, www.eta.co.uk, www.nytimes.com, Bridgestone Teens Drive Smart:
Young Drivers Survey April 2012, www.usatoday.com

*Although every effort has been made to trace and contact copyright holders before
publication, this has not been possible in some cases. We apologize for any apparent
infringement of copyright and, if notified, the publisher will be pleased to rectify any
errors or omissions at the earliest possible opportunity.*

Illustrations by: Cover: Chellie Carroll; Dutch Uncle Agency/Atsushi Hara pp.4, 9,
14, 21, 31, 42, 44; Good Illustration/Oliver Latyk p.51; Tim Marrs pp.22, 61;
New Division/Anna Hymas p.33, 41; Organisation/Fred Van Deelan p.46;
Roger Penwill p.18, 43; Martin Sanders p.19.

*The publisher would like to thank the following for their kind permission to reproduce
photographs*: **COVER**: Gemenacom/shutterstock.com, Andrey_Popov/
shutterstock.com, Wavebreakmedia/shutterstock.com, Image Source/Getty
Images, Lane Oatey/Blue Jean Images/Getty Images, BJI/Blue Jean Images/Getty
Images, Image Source/Corbis, Yuri Arcurs/Tetra Images/Corbis, Wavebreak
Media Ltd./Corbis; **ALAMY**: pp.7 (Robert Harding Picture Library/Chart), 12
(MBI/Doctor), 16 (Senarb Commercial), 17 (Tony Hobbs/cockpit, Jack Sullivan/
passengers), 25 (Tristan Deschamps/beach house), 27 (Chris Rout), 30 (Jason
O.Watson), 41 (ZImages), 59 (Mike Goldwater/street scene), 65 (glasses), 67
(Batchelder/ central park), 54 (Jeff Greenberg 5 of 6/journalists); **C. BLACKIE**:
p.8; **CORBIS**: pp.5 (C.Masur/F1), 6 (Wavebreak Media Ltd.), 20 (Rune Hellestad/
Michael Morpurgo), 23 (Tracey Lee), 25 (Helen King/man on train), 32
(Bill Stormont/firefighter), 52 (Image Source/police officer), 60 (David P Hall);
DART CONTAINER CORPORATION: p.64 (drinks carton); **FOTOLIA**: p. 24
(storm/firefighter); **GETTY IMAGES**: pp.7 (Glen Allison/fabric, Sunita Menon/
India Today Group), 11 (Jon Feingers/shaving), (Stewart Cohen/woman
reading), (Brian Leatart/roast turkey), 15 (kparis/woman in café), (Visit Britain/
Pawel Libera/shop), 17 (Donald M. Jones/Sea otter), 18 (John Lund/aircraft),
20 (WireImage/Suzanne Collins, Haruki Marakami), 24 (Estate of Stephen
Laurence Strathdee/aeroplane) , (David De Lossy/footprints), 25 (Dougal Water/
cracked earth), (Blend Images/Ariel Skelley/conference), (Luis Pelaez Inc/
making lunch), (Gary S Chapman/woman studying), 28 (Peathegee Inc), 29
(Matej Michelizza), 34 (Seattle Dredge), 37 (Future Publishing/concert), (Image
Source/boy with headphones), 35 (Tetra Images/couple on couch), 38 (Dave
King/keyboard, Rhythm Magazine/drums), (WireImage/conductor), (Greg Dale/
Cello, Tetra Images/Bass guitar), 39 (playing trombone, SSPL/dancing), p.43
(Mint Images – Tim Pannell/street), 47 (Compassionate Eye Foundation/Chris
Windsor), 49, 55 (car and felled tree), 56, 59 (Blackstation/Shanghai city), 64
(Thomas Lehmann/cans), (Peter Dazeley/cashpoint), (C Squared Studios/paper
bag), (David Bishop Inc/lollipops), 65 (John Lamb/ear test), (Steven Puetzer/
smoke detector), 67 (AFP/toy shop), (De Agostini/Bersezio/Mt Everest), (Nigel
Pavitt/Lake Victoria), (Gonzalo Azumendi Collection/Panama canal), (Gonzalo
Azumendi/Balearic Islands), (David McNew/freeway); **KOBAL COLLECTION**:
p.48 (MDP/New Market/Page, Gene/Charlize Theron); **OXFORD UNIVERSITY
PRESS PICTUREBANK**: p.50, 52 (fingerprint, wallet, phone, purse, Mp3
player, handcuffs), 67 (flag); **THE PORT AUTHORITY OF NEW YORK AND
NEW JERSEY**: p.17 (turtle); **PRESS ASSOCIATION IMAGES**: p.26 (Thomas
Frey/DPA/Ewa Wisnierska), 36 , 39 (woman with earphones), 67 (AP/Edmund
Hillary), 68; **REX FEATURES**: pp.10, 11 (Henrik5000/brain), 20 (David Hartley/
Philip Pullman), 48 (Everett/Dreamworks/20th Century Fox/Daniel Day Lewis),
53 (PDN/Villard/Sipa), 55 (weather man, Mike Forster/Associated Newspapers/
street scene), 62 (AMC/Everett Collection), 66 (Everett Collection/Sacheen
Littlefeather and Parmount/Marlon Brando); **SHUTTERSTOCK**: p.37 (hearing
aid) 38 (violin, saxophone, orchestra, soprano, choir, flute), 42 (notebook).